Serverless Design Patterns and Best Practices

Build, secure, and deploy enterprise ready serverless
applications with AWS to improve developer productivity

Brian Zambrano

BIRMINGHAM - MUMBAI

Serverless Design Patterns and Best Practices

Copyright © 2018 Packt Publishing

Commissioning Editor: Richa Tripathi
Acquisition Editor: Sandeep Mishra
Content Development Editor: Akshada Iyer
Technical Editor: Mehul Singh
Copy Editor: Safis Editing
Project Coordinator: Prajakta Naik
Proofreader: Safis Editing
Indexer: Rekha Nair
Graphics: Jisha Chirayil
Production Coordinator: Shraddha Falebhai

First published: April 2018

Production reference: 1110418

Published by Packt Publishing Ltd.
Livery Place
35 Livery Street
Birmingham
B3 2PB, UK.

ISBN 978-1-78862-064-2

www.packtpub.com

To my parents, who put me above everything else to help make me who I am today

mapt.io

Mapt is an online digital library that gives you full access to over 5,000 books and videos, as well as industry leading tools to help you plan your personal development and advance your career. For more information, please visit our website.

Why subscribe?

- Spend less time learning and more time coding with practical eBooks and Videos from over 4,000 industry professionals

- Improve your learning with Skill Plans built especially for you

- Get a free eBook or video every month

- Mapt is fully searchable

- Copy and paste, print, and bookmark content

PacktPub.com

Did you know that Packt offers eBook versions of every book published, with PDF and ePub files available? You can upgrade to the eBook version at www.PacktPub.com and as a print book customer, you are entitled to a discount on the eBook copy. Get in touch with us at service@packtpub.com for more details.

At www.PacktPub.com, you can also read a collection of free technical articles, sign up for a range of free newsletters, and receive exclusive discounts and offers on Packt books and eBooks.

Contributors

About the author

Brian Zambrano is a software engineer and architect with a background cloud-based SAAS application architecture, design, and scalability. Brian has been working with AWS consistently since 2009. For the past several years, he has focused on cloud architecture with AWS using serverless technologies, microservices, containers, and the vast array of AWS services.

Brian was born and bred in the San Francisco Bay Area and currently resides in Fort Collins, CO with his wife and twin boys.

I'm grateful to my wife, who was encouraging in spite of my many late nights and weekend days sitting in front of the computer. Thanks very much to my team at Very, LLC for their encouragement and giving me Fridays to write this book. A special thanks to my colleague Daniel Searles, who took the time to be a technical reviewer, providing valuable feedback.

About the reviewer

Daniel Paul Searles enthusiastically attempted to learn to program by book at thirteen, only to be completely stumped by a technical error in one of the required coding exercises. A number of years later, he was successful with another book, which propelled him to gain experience across many languages, operating systems, and tech stacks. The thought of what could have been if he was able to learn to program at a younger age energizes his work as a technical reviewer. Currently, he is pursuing Machine Learning and Functional Programming.

Packt is searching for authors like you

If you're interested in becoming an author for Packt, please visit `authors.packtpub.com` and apply today. We have worked with thousands of developers and tech professionals, just like you, to help them share their insight with the global tech community. You can make a general application, apply for a specific hot topic that we are recruiting an author for, or submit your own idea.

Table of Contents

Preface   1

Chapter 1: Introduction   7
  What is serverless computing?   8
    No servers to manage   8
    Pay-per-invocation billing model   9
    Ability to automatically scale with usage   10
    Built-in availability and fault tolerance   10
  Design patterns   11
  When to use serverless   12
    The sweet spot   12
  Classes of serverless pattern   13
    Three-tier web application patterns   13
    ETL patterns   14
    Big data patterns   15
    Automation and deployment patterns   16
  Serverless frameworks   16
  Summary   17

Chapter 2: A Three-Tier Web Application Using REST   19
  Serverless tooling   20
  System architecture   21
    Presentation layer   23
    Logic layer   23
    Data layer   23
  Logic layer   23
    Application code and function layout   23
      Organization of the Lambda functions   24
      Organization of the application code   25
    Configuration with environment variables   26
    Code structure   26
    Function layout   28
  Presentation layer   29
    File storage with S3   29
    CDN with CloudFront   30
  Data layer   30
  Writing our logic layer   30
    Application entrypoint   31
    Application logic   33
    Wiring handler.py to Lambda via API Gateway   36

Deploying the REST API   37
Deploying the Postgres database   39
Setting up static assets   41
Viewing the deployed web application   43
Running tests   44
Iteration and deployment   47
     Deploying the entire stack   47
     Deploying the application code   48
Summary   49

Chapter 3: A Three-Tier Web Application Pattern with GraphQL   51
Introduction to GraphQL   52
System architecture   53
Logic layer   54
     Organization of the Lambda functions   54
     Organization of the application code   56
     Function layout   57
Presentation layer   57
Writing the logic layer   58
     Implementing the entry point   59
     Implementing GraphQL queries   59
     Implementing GraphQL mutations   63
Deployment   64
Viewing the deployed application   66
Iteration and deployment   72
Summary   73

Chapter 4: Integrating Legacy APIs with the Proxy Pattern   75
AWS API Gateway introduction   76
Simple proxy to a legacy API   77
     Setting up a pass-through proxy   78
     Deploying a pass-through proxy   81
Transforming responses from a modern API   83
     Method execution flow   84
     Setting up example   86
     Setting up a new resource and method   87
     Setting up Integration Request   88
     Setting up Integration Response   90
Complex integration using a Lambda function   93
     Implementing the application code   94
     Setting up a new resource and method   96
Migration techniques   97
     Staged migration   98
     Migrating URLs   99

Summary	100
Chapter 5: Scaling Out with the Fan-Out Pattern	101
System architecture	102
Synchronous versus asynchronous invocation	103
Resizing images in parallel	104
Setting up the project	104
Setting up trigger and worker functions	105
Setting up permissions	106
Implementing the application code	107
Testing our code	110
Alternate Implementations	113
Using notifications with subscriptions	113
Using notifications with queues	115
Summary	116
Chapter 6: Asynchronous Processing with the Messaging Pattern	117
Basics of queuing systems	118
Choosing a queue service	119
Queues versus streams	120
Asynchronous processing of Twitter streams	122
System architecture	122
Data producer	124
Mimicking daemon processes with serverless functions	126
Data consumers	128
Viewing results	133
Alternate Implementations	134
Using the Fan-out and Messaging Patterns together	134
Using a queue as a rate-limiter	135
Using a dead-letter queue	137
Summary	138
Chapter 7: Data Processing Using the Lambda Pattern	139
Introducing the lambda architecture	140
Batch layer	142
Speed layer	143
Lambda serverless architecture	143
Streaming data producers	144
Data storage	144
Computation in the speed layer	145
Computation in the batch layer	146
Processing cryptocurrency prices using lambda architecture	146
System architecture	147
Data producer	148
Speed layer	148
Batch layer	148

AWS resources   149
Data producer   154
Speed layer   156
Batch layer   158
Results   162
Summary   164
Chapter 8: The MapReduce Pattern   167
Introduction to MapReduce   168
MapReduce example   168
Role of the mapper   170
Role of the reducer   171
MapReduce architecture   171
MapReduce serverless architecture   173
Processing Enron emails with serverless MapReduce   175
Driver function   176
Mapper implementation   178
Reducer implementation   180
Understanding the limitations of serverless MapReduce   185
Memory limits   185
Storage limits   186
Time limits   187
Exploring alternate implementations   187
AWS Athena   187
Using a data store for results   189
Using Elastic MapReduce   191
Summary   192
Chapter 9: Deployment and CI/CD Patterns   193
Introduction to CI/CD   194
CI   194
CD   194
Setting up unit tests   195
Code organization   196
Setting up unit tests   197
Setting up CI with CircleCI   199
Configuring CircleCI builds   200
Setting up environment variables   203
Setting up CD and deployments with CircleCI   204
Setting up Slack notifications   204
Setting up a CircleCI badge   206
Setting up deployments   206
Setting up AWS credentials   206
Setting up environment variables   207
Executing deployments   209

Summary	214
Chapter 10: Error Handling and Best Practices	215
Error tracking	216
Integrating Sentry for error tracking	216
Integrating Rollbar	222
Logging	223
Structuring log messages	223
Digesting structured logs	225
Cold starts	226
Keeping cloud functions warm	226
AWS Lambda functions and VPCs	227
Start-up times for different languages	227
Allocating more memory	228
Local development and testing	228
Local development	228
Learning about testing locally	229
Managing different environments	231
Securing sensitive configuration	232
Encrypting variables	233
Decrypting variables	235
Trimming AWS Lambda versions	236
Summary	238
Other Books You May Enjoy	239
Index	243

Preface

Serverless architectures are changing the way software systems are being built and operated. When compared with systems that use physical servers or virtual machines, many tools, techniques, and patterns remain the same; however, there are several things that can or need to change drastically. To fully capitalize on the benefits of serverless systems, tools, patterns, and best practices should be thought through carefully before embarking on a serverless journey.

This book introduces and describes reusable patterns applicable to almost any type of serverless application, whether it be web systems, data processing, big data, or Internet of Things. You will learn, by example and explanation, about various patterns within a serverless context, such as RESTful APIs, GraphQL, proxy, fan-out, messaging, lambda architecture, and MapReduce, as well as when to use these patterns to make your applications scalable, performant, and fault tolerant. This book will take you through techniques for Continuous Integration and Continuous Deployment as well as designs for testing, securing, and scaling your serverless applications. Learning and applying these patterns will speed up your development lifecycle, while also improving the overall application architecture when building on top of your serverless platform of choice.

Who this book is for

This book is aimed at software engineers, architects, and anyone who is interested in building serverless applications using a cloud provider. Readers should be interested in learning popular patterns to improve agility, code quality, and performance, while also avoiding some of the pitfalls that new users may fall into when starting with serverless systems. Programming knowledge and basic serverless computing concepts are assumed.

What this book covers

Chapter 1, *Introduction*, covers the basics of serverless systems and discusses when serverless architectures may or may not be a good fit. Three categories of serverless patterns are introduced and briefly explained.

Chapter 2, *A Three-Tier Web Application Using REST,* walks you through a full example of building a traditional web application using a REST API powered by AWS Lambda, along with serverless technologies for hosting HTML, CSS, and JavaScript for the frontend code.

Chapter 3, *A Three-Tier Web Application Pattern with GraphQL,* introduces GraphQL and explains the changes needed to turn the previous REST API into a GraphQL API.

Chapter 4, *Integrating Legacy APIs with the Proxy Pattern,* demonstrates how it's possible to completely change an API contract while using a legacy API backend using nothing other than AWS API Gateway.

Chapter 5, *Scaling Out with the Fan-Out Pattern,* teaches you one of the most basic serverless patterns around, where a single event triggers multiple parallel serverless functions, resulting in quicker execution times over a serial implementation.

Chapter 6, *Asynchronous Processing with the Messaging Pattern,* explains different classes of messaging patterns and demonstrates how to put messages onto a queue using a serverless data producer, and process those messages downstream with a serverless data consumer.

Chapter 7, *Data Processing Using the Lambda Pattern,* explains how you can use multiple subpatterns to create two planes of computation, which provide views into historical aggregated data as well as real-time data.

Chapter 8, *The MapReduce Pattern,* explores an example implementation of aggregating large volumes of data in parallel, similar to the way systems such as Hadoop work.

Chapter 9, *Deployment and CI/CD Patterns,* explain how to set up Continuous Integration and Continuous Delivery for serverless projects and what to keep in mind when doing so, in addition to showing examples of continuous deployment.

Chapter 10, *Error Handling and Best Practices,* reviews the tools and techniques for automatically tracking unexpected errors as well as several best practices and tips when creating serverless applications.

To get the most out of this book

1. Almost all of the examples in this book use the Serverless Framework to manage AWS resources and Lambda functions. Installation instructions for the Serverless Framework can be found at https://serverless.com/framework/docs/getting-started/.

2. In addition to the Serverless Framework, readers will need to have an AWS account to run the examples. For those new to AWS, you can create a new account, which comes with a year of usage in their Free Tier, at https://aws.amazon.com.

   During the course of this book, you will need the following tools:

   - AWS Lambda
   - AWS RDS
   - AWS API Gateway
   - AWS DynamoDB
   - AWS S3
   - AWS SQS
   - AWS Rekognition
   - AWS Kinesis
   - AWS SNS

   We will learn how to use these tools through the course of this book.

Download the example code files

You can download the example code files for this book from your account at www.packtpub.com. If you purchased this book elsewhere, you can visit www.packtpub.com/support and register to have the files emailed directly to you.

You can download the code files by following these steps:

1. Log in or register at www.packtpub.com.
2. Select the **SUPPORT** tab.
3. Click on **Code Downloads & Errata**.
4. Enter the name of the book in the **Search** box and follow the onscreen instructions.

Once the file is downloaded, please make sure that you unzip or extract the folder using the latest version of:

- WinRAR/7-Zip for Windows
- Zipeg/iZip/UnRarX for Mac
- 7-Zip/PeaZip for Linux

The code bundle for the book is also hosted on GitHub at https://github.com/ PacktPublishing/Serverless-Design-Patterns-and-Best-Practices. In case there's an update to the code, it will be updated on the existing GitHub repository.

We also have other code bundles from our rich catalog of books and videos available at https://github.com/PacktPublishing/. Check them out!

Conventions used

There are a number of text conventions used throughout this book.

CodeInText: Indicates code words in text, database table names, folder names, filenames, file extensions, pathnames, dummy URLs, user input, and Twitter handles. Here is an example: "To test this, we need to set the timeout of the divide function to 4 seconds and put a time.sleep(3) in the middle of the application code."

A block of code is set as follows:

```
def divide(event, context):
    params = event.get('queryStringParameters') or {}
    numerator = int(params.get('numerator', 10))
    denominator = int(params.get('denominator', 2))
    body = {
        "message": "Results of %s / %s = %s" % (
            numerator,
            denominator,
            numerator // denominator,
        )
    }

    response = {
        "statusCode": 200,
        "body": json.dumps(body)
    }

    return response
```

When we wish to draw your attention to a particular part of a code block, the relevant lines or items are set in bold:

```
from raven_python_lambda import RavenLambdaWrapper

@RavenLambdaWrapper()

from raven_python_lambda import RavenLambdaWrapper

@RavenLambdaWrapper()
def divide(event, context):
    # Code
```

Any command-line input or output is written as follows:

```
$ curl
"https://5gj9zthyv1.execute-api.us-west-2.amazonaws.com/dev?numerator=12&denominator=3"
{"message": "Results of 12 / 3 = 4"}
```

Bold: Indicates a new term, an important word, or words that you see onscreen. For example, words in menus or dialog boxes appear in the text like this. Here is an example: "The following screenshot shows **Invocation errors** from the AWS Lambda monitoring page for the divide function:"

Warnings or important notes appear like this.

Tips and tricks appear like this.

Get in touch

Feedback from our readers is always welcome.

General feedback: Email feedback@packtpub.com and mention the book title in the subject of your message. If you have questions about any aspect of this book, please email us at questions@packtpub.com.

Errata: Although we have taken every care to ensure the accuracy of our content, mistakes do happen. If you have found a mistake in this book, we would be grateful if you would report this to us. Please visit www.packtpub.com/submit-errata, selecting your book, clicking on the Errata Submission Form link, and entering the details.

Piracy: If you come across any illegal copies of our works in any form on the Internet, we would be grateful if you would provide us with the location address or website name. Please contact us at copyright@packtpub.com with a link to the material.

If you are interested in becoming an author: If there is a topic that you have expertise in and you are interested in either writing or contributing to a book, please visit authors.packtpub.com.

Reviews

Please leave a review. Once you have read and used this book, why not leave a review on the site that you purchased it from? Potential readers can then see and use your unbiased opinion to make purchase decisions, we at Packt can understand what you think about our products, and our authors can see your feedback on their book. Thank you!

For more information about Packt, please visit packtpub.com.

Introduction 1

It's an exciting time to be in the software industry. Over the past few years, we've seen an evolution in architectural patterns, with a considerable movement away from large, monolithic applications toward microservices. As cloud computing has evolved, so too have the systems and services we software developers have at our disposal. One of the most revolutionary tools in this domain is lambda functions, or more accurately, Functions as a Service. A step beyond microservices, being able to run, manage, and deploy a single function as a different entity has pushed us into the realm of nanoservices.

Of course, this book focuses on design patterns for serverless computing. The best place to start then is: what are design patterns and what is serverless computing?

If you're just beginning your journey into the world of serverless systems and patterns, I encourage you to read other resources to get more details on these and related topics. Our upcoming discussion intends to set the stage for building systems with patterns, but it's not necessary to explain the foundations of serverless platforms or its concepts in excruciating detail.

In this chapter, I'll first define a few relevant terms and concepts before diving deeper into those topics. Then, I'll discuss when serverless architectures are or are not a good fit. Finally, I'll explain the various categories of serverless patterns that I'll present in this book. I presume that you, the reader, are somewhat familiar with these large topics, but absolute mastery is not required.

At the end of this chapter, you should be able to do the following:

- Describe the term *serverless* in your own words
- Know how design patterns relate to serverless architectures
- Understand general classifications of serverless design patterns

What is serverless computing?

Let's start with the simpler of the two questions first—what is serverless computing? While there may be several ways to define serverless computing, or perhaps more accurately serverless architectures, most people can agree on a few key attributes. Serverless computing platforms share the following features:

- No operating systems to configure or manage
- Pay-per-invocation billing model
- Ability to automatically scale with usage
- Built-in availability and fault tolerance

While there are other attributes that come with serverless platforms, they all share these common traits. Additionally, there are other serverless systems that provide functionality other than general computing power. Examples of these are DynamoDB, Kinesis, and Simple Queue Service, all of which fall under the Amazon Web Services (AWS) umbrella. Even though these systems are not pay-per-invocation, they fall into the serverless category since the management of the underlying systems is delegated to the AWS team, scaling is a matter of changing a few settings, fault-tolerance is built-in, and high availability is handled automatically.

No servers to manage

Arguably, this is where the term *serverless* came from and is at the heart of this entire movement. If we look back not too long ago, we can see a time when operations teams had to purchase physical hardware, mount it in a data center, and configure it. All of this was required before engineers even had the chance of deploying their software.

Cloud computing, of course, revolutionized this process and turned it upside down, putting individual engineers in the driver's seat. With a few clicks or API calls, we could now get our very own **virtual private server** (**VPS**) in minutes rather than weeks or months. While this was and is incredibly enabling, most of the work of setting up systems remained. A short list of things to worry about includes the following:

- Updating the operating system
- Securing the operating system
- Installing system packages
- Dealing with dependency management

This list goes on and on. A point worth noting is that there may be hours and hours of configuration and management before we're in a position to deploy and test our software.

To ease the burden of system setup, configuration software such as Puppet, Chef, SaltStack, and Ansible arrived on the scene. Again, these were and are incredibly enabling. Once you have your recipes in place, configuring a new virtual host is, most importantly, repeatable and hopefully less error-prone than doing a manual setup. In systems that comprise hundreds or even thousands of virtual servers, some automation is a requirement rather than a mere convenience.

As lovely as these provisioning tools are, they do come with a significant cost of ownership and can be incredibly time-consuming to develop and maintain. Often, iterating on this infrastructure-as-code tooling requires making changes and then executing them. Starting up a new virtual host is orders of magnitude faster than setting up a physical server; however, we measure VPS boot time and provisioning time in minutes. Additionally, these are software systems in and of themselves that a dedicated team needs to learn, test, debug, and maintain. On top of this, you need to continually maintain and update provisioning tools and scripts in parallel with any changes to your operating systems. If you wanted to change the base operating system, it would be possible but not without significant investment and updates to your existing code.

When Lambda was launched by AWS in 2014, a new paradigm for computing and software management was born. In contrast to managing your virtual hosts, AWS Lambda provided developers the ability to deploy application code in a managed environment without needing to manage virtual hosts themselves. Of course, there are servers running somewhere that are operated by someone. However, the details of these servers are opaque to us as application developers. No longer do we need to worry about the operating system and its configuration directly. With AWS Lambda and other Functions as a Service (FaaS) platforms, we can now delegate the work of VPS management to the teams behind those platforms.

The most significant shift in thinking with FaaS platforms is that the unit of measure has shrunk from a virtual machine to a single function.

Pay-per-invocation billing model

Another significant change with the invention of serverless platforms is the pay-per-invocation model. Before this, billing models were typically per minute or hour. While this was the backbone of elastic computing, servers needed to stay up and running if they were used in any production environment.

Paying for a VPS only while it's running is a great model when developing since you can just start it at the beginning of the day and terminate it at the end of the day. However, when a system needs to be available all the time, the price you pay is nearly the same whether its CPU is at 100% usage or 0.0001% usage.

Serverless platforms, on the other hand, the bill only while the code is being executed. They are designed and shine for systems that are stateless and have a finite, relatively short duration. As such, billing is typically calculated based on a total invocation time. This model works exceptionally well for smaller systems that may get only a few calls or invocations per day. On many platforms, it's possible to run a production system that is always available completely for free. There is no such thing as idle time in the world of serverless.

Ability to automatically scale with usage

Gone are the days of needing to overprovision a system with more virtual hosts than you typically need. As invocations ramp up, the underlying system automatically scales up, providing you with a known number of concurrent invocations. Moving this limit higher is merely a matter of making a support request to Amazon, in the case of AWS Lambda. Before this, managing horizontal scalability was an exercise for the team designing the system. Never has horizontal scalability for computing resources been so easy.

Different cloud providers provide the ability to scale up or down (that is, be elastic) based on various parameters and metrics. Talk to DevOps folks or engineers who run systems with autoscaling and they will tell you it's not a trivial matter and is difficult to get right.

Built-in availability and fault tolerance

Servers, real or virtual, can and do fail. Since the hosts that run your code are now of little or no concern for you, it's a worry not worth having.

Just as the management of the operating system is handled for you, so too is the management of failing servers. You can be guaranteed that when your application code should be invoked, it will be.

Design patterns

With a good understanding of serverless computing behind us, let's turn our attention to design patterns.

If you've spent any amount of time working with software, you will have heard the term *design pattern* and may very well be familiar with them to some degree. Stepping back slightly, let's discuss what a design pattern is.

I will assert that if you ask 10 different developers to define the term *design pattern*, you will get 10 different answers. While we all may have our definition, and while those definitions may not be wrong, it's relatively simple to agree on the general spirit or idea of a software design pattern. Within the context of software engineering, design patterns are reusable solutions or code organization applied to a frequently occurring problem. For example, the Model-View-Controller pattern evolved to solve the problem of GUI applications. The Model-View-Controller pattern can be implemented in almost any language for nearly any GUI application.

Software design patterns evolved as a solution to help software authors be more efficient by applying well-known and proven templates to their application code. Likewise, architectural patterns provide the same benefits but at the level of the overall system design, rather than at the code level.

In this book, we won't be focusing on software design, but rather architectural design in serverless systems. In that vein, it's worth noting that the context of this book is serverless architectures and our patterns will manifest themselves as reusable solutions that you can use to organize your functions and other computing resources to solve various types of problem on your serverless platform of choice.

Of course, there is an infinite number of ways to organize your application code and hundreds of software and architectural patterns you can use. The primary focus here is the general organization or grouping of your functions, how they interact with one another, the roles and responsibilities of each function, and how they operate in isolation but work together to compose a larger and more complex system.

As serverless systems gain traction and become more and more popular, I would expect serverless patterns such as those we will discuss in this book to grow in both popularity and number.

When to use serverless

Many types of computing problem can be solved with a serverless design. Personally speaking, I have a hard time not using serverless systems nowadays due to the speed, flexibility, and adaptability they provide. The classes of problem that are suitable for serverless systems are extensive. Still, there is a sweet spot that is good to keep in mind when approaching new problems. Outside of the sweet spot, there are problems that are not a good fit.

The sweet spot

Since serverless systems work on the basis of a single function, they are well suited to problems that are, or can be broken down into, the following subsystems:

- Stateless
- Computationally small and predictable

Serverless functions are ephemeral; that is, they have a known lifetime. Computation that is itself stateless is the type of problem where FaaS platforms shine. Application state may exist, and functions may store that state using a database or some other kind of data store, but the functions themselves retain no state between invocations.

In terms of computing resources, serverless functions have an upper bound, both in memory and total duration. Your software should have an expected or predictable upper limit that is below that of your FaaS provider. At the time of writing, AWS Lambda functions have an upper bound of 1,536 MB for memory and 300 seconds in duration. Google Compute advertises an upper limit of 540 seconds. Regardless of the actual values, systems, where you can reliably play within these bounds, are good candidates for moving to serverless architecture.

A good, albeit trivial, an example of this would be a data transformation function—given some input data, transform it into a different data structure. It should be clear with such a simple example that no state needs to be or is carried between one invocation and the next. Of course, data comes in various sizes, but if your system is fed data of a predictable size, you should be able to process the data within a certain timeframe.

In contrast, long-running processes that share state are not good fits for serverless. The reason for this is that functions die at the end of their life, leaving any in-memory state to die with them. Imagine a long-running process such as an application server handling WebSocket connections.

WebSockets are, by definition, stateful and can be compared to a phone call—a client opens up a connection to a server that is kept open as long as the client would like. Scenarios such as this are not a good fit for serverless functions for the two following reasons:

- State exists (i.e., state of a phone call is connected or disconnected)
- The process is long-lived because the connection can remain open for hours or days

Whenever I approach a new problem and begin to consider serverless, I ask myself these two questions:

- Is there any global state involved that needs to be kept track of within the application code?
- Is the computation to be performed beyond the system limits of my serverless platform?

The good news is that, very often, the answer to these questions is no and I can move forward and build my application using a serverless architecture.

Classes of serverless pattern

In this book, we'll discuss four major classes of serverless design pattern:

- Three-tier web application patterns
- **Extract**, **transform**, **load** (ETL) patterns
- Big data patterns
- Automation and deployment patterns

Three-tier web application patterns

Web applications with the traditional request/response cycle are a sweet spot for serverless systems. Because serverless functions are short-lived, they lend themselves well to problems that are themselves short-lived and stateless. We have seen stateful systems emerge and become popular, such as WebSockets; however, much of the web and web applications still run in the traditional stateless request/response cycle. In our first set of patterns, we'll build different versions of web application APIs.

While there are three different patterns to cover for web applications, they will all share a common basis, which is the three-tier model. Here, the tiers are made up of the following:

- Content Delivery Network (CDN) for presentation code/static assets (HTML, JavaScript, CSS, and so on)
- Database for persistence
- Serverless functions for application logic

REST APIs should be a common and familiar tool for most web developers. In Chapter 2, *A Three-Tier Web Application Using REST*, we'll build out a fully featured REST API with a serverless design. This API will have all of the methods you'd expect in a classic REST API—**create, read, update, delete (CRUD)**.

While REST APIs are common and well understood, they do face some challenges. After starting with a serverless REST API, we'll walk through the process of designing the changes needed to make that same API work as a single GraphQL endpoint that provides the same functionality in Chapter 3, *A Three-Tier Web Application Pattern with GraphQL*.

Finally, in Chapter 4, *Integrating Legacy APIs with the Proxy Pattern*, we'll use a proxy pattern to show how it's possible to completely change an API but use a legacy API backend. This design is especially interesting for those who would like to get started migrating an API to a serverless platform but have an existing API to maintain.

ETL patterns

ETL patterns is another area of computing that lends itself very well to serverless platforms. At a high level, ETL jobs comprise the following three steps:

- Extracting data from one data source
- Transforming that data appropriately
- Loading the processed data into another data source

Often used in analytics and/or data warehousing, ETL jobs are hard to escape. Since this problem is again ephemeral and because users would probably like their ETL jobs to execute as quickly as possible, serverless systems are a great platform in this problem space. While serverless computation is typically short-lived, we will see how ETL processes can be designed to be long-running in order to work through large amounts of data.

In the fan-out pattern, discussed in Chapter 5, *Scaling Out with the Fan-Out Pattern*, a single unit of work will be broken up into multiple smaller units of work and processed in parallel. This pattern may be used as a standalone system or as a subcomponent in a more extensive system. We'll build out an application using the fan-out pattern in isolation, but later discuss how it can work as a piece in a more extensive system.

Messaging patterns themselves can be an entire class of design pattern. In our context, we will show how to use this as a general pattern to process data asynchronously with a known or fixed amount of processing power. Chapter 6, *Asynchronous Processing with the Messaging Pattern*, will walk through a full example of this pattern and its variants in a serverless context.

Big data patterns

It may seem confusing that *lambda* can refer to both AWS Lambda functions as well as a pattern in and of itself. The lambda pattern was born from the need to analyze large amounts of data in real time. Before this, the big data movement, where large batch jobs would run to calculate and recalculate things, was in full swing. The problem faced by this movement was that these batch jobs, in order to get the latest results, would need to spend the majority of their computing resources recalculating metrics on data that hadn't changed.

The lambda pattern, which we will discuss in Chapter 7, *Data Processing Using the Lambda Pattern*, creates two parallel planes of computation, a batch layer, and a speed layer. The naming of these layers should give you an idea of what they're responsible for.

MapReduce is another well-known and tested paradigm that has been popular in the software world for some time now. Hadoop, arguably the most famous framework for MapReduce, helped to bring this pattern front and center after Google's original MapReduce paper in 2004.

As amazing as Hadoop is as a software system, there are substantial hurdles to overcome in running a production Hadoop cluster of your own. Due to this, systems such as Amazon's **Elastic MapReduce (EMR)** were developed, which provide on-demand Hadoop jobs to the developer. Still, authoring Hadoop jobs and managing the underlying computing resources can be non-trivial. We'll walk through writing your serverless MapReduce system in Chapter 8, *MapReduce Pattern*.

Automation and deployment patterns

Many of us are used to logging onto a machine via `ssh` and grepping through log files to look for problems. Our worlds are now turned upside down since there are no longer any servers to SSH into. Fortunately, there are methods of handling errors and getting the information needed to debug and monitor your programs.

In `Chapter 9`, *Deployment and CI/CD Patterns*, we'll focus on error handling, as well as some of the dos and don'ts of serverless systems and what modern-day best practices look like in the serverless world. Many development practices change when building on top of a serverless platform and there are a lot of gotchas that, if you're unfamiliar with them, may surprise you. `Chapter 9`, *Deployment and CI/CD Patterns*, will walk through some of the biggest issues that may bite you if you're brand new to this ecosystem.

While some tooling and techniques may change, let's not forget a healthy software development life cycle consists of well-structured code, **continuous integration (CI)**, **continuous deployment (CD)**, and unit tests. Coupled with the myriad of hosted CI/CD platforms, running tests and deploying code automatically is quite painless and even fun. In `Chapter 10`, *Deployment and CI/CD Patterns* will discuss various options and examples with hosted CI and CD platforms. I'm confident that you'll find the velocity at which you can ship code using serverless technologies exciting and enabling.

Serverless frameworks

With the advent of serverless platforms came the creation of multiple frameworks to help us manage our serverless applications. Just as Ruby on Rails, Spring, Django, Express, and other web frameworks aid in the creation and management of web applications, various serverless frameworks have sprung up that make the software development lifecycle easier for serverless applications.

An essential difference between web frameworks and serverless frameworks is that serverless frameworks often help with the management of application code on a serverless platform. In contrast, much of the help web frameworks provide revolves around web logic and tasks such as the following:

- Producing HTML output via templating engines
- Managing database records via Object Relational Mappers (ORMs)
- Validating submitted form data
- Dealing with the details of HTTP requests and responses

Not all applications that run on a serverless platform are HTTP-based. Therefore, serverless frameworks do not necessarily have application-specific functionality baked in but, instead, they have deployment and management functionality. Some frameworks do target web developers and aid in web-centric tasks; however, there are several other frameworks that do not and instead focus on managing arbitrary application code.

A few popular serverless frameworks worth noting are the following:

- Apex
- Serverless
- ClaudiaJS
- Kappa
- SAM (Serverless Application Model from AWS)
- Chalice (from AWS)
- Zappa

Throughout this book, I'll be using a serverless framework to manage application code and the entire stack of resources that we will deploy during the examples. Serverless works with a variety of programming languages and various platforms, such as AWS, Azure, Google Compute Cloud, and IBM Open Whisk. We will build all of our examples using AWS, but the patterns discussed should apply to other cloud providers unless explicitly noted otherwise. Since serverless frameworks such as Zappa don't give us any web-specific functionality, we will be responsible for some of the lower-level web application details in Chapter 2, *A Three-Tier Web Application Using REST,* and Chapter 3, *A Three-Tier Web Application Pattern with GraphQL.*

Summary

In this introduction, we covered the main points regarding serverless platforms and discussed the attributes that make a system *serverless.* We covered the main differences between building software on top of self-managed systems, either physical or virtual, compared to building software systems on a serverless platform. Additionally, readers should have a clearer perspective of when serverless architectures are a good fit and when they are not.

We also reviewed the main categories of design pattern that I will cover in this book and gained a high-level overview of each one. Finally, I covered the differences between web and serverless frameworks and gave some examples of the latter.

With the stage set, we can jump into our first pattern with a real-world example. By the end of Chapter 2, *A Three-Tier Web Application Using REST*, we will have produced a complete three-tier web application using REST API, all with serverless technologies.

A Three-Tier Web Application Using REST

2

It should be safe to say that the vast majority of developers know what REST is. A three-tier web application consists of the following:

- Presentation layer (HTML and CSS)
- Business logic layer (application code)
- Data layer (Relational Database Management System or another type of data store)

The three-tier web application is extremely well known and one of the most common designs on the web today. Readers are likely familiar with this design when thinking about a web application's static content (that is, HTML, JavaScript, and CSS) which are served from a **content delivery network** (**CDN**), which talks to a RESTful API hosted on a web server, which, in turn, talks to a database.

In this chapter, we will go through the process of building a three-tier web application using HTML, JavaScript, and CSS for our presentation layer, a REST API for our business logic, and a Postgres database for our data tier. Most importantly, and keeping in line with this book, this will all be accomplished using serverless technologies or services where you do not need to manage servers yourself.

By the end of this chapter, you can expect to know the following:

- How to author a REST API using **Amazon Web Services** (**AWS**) Lambda and Python
- How to build, manage, and deploy static assets to a CDN
- How to create and maintain an RDS Postgres database
- Options for designing RESTful APIs, including different languages, frameworks, and layouts of functions

- Static asset life cycle management and caching for optimal performance

Serverless tooling

Since this is the very first chapter that has application code and working examples, it's important to talk through some of the tooling and systems to set the stage for this and subsequent chapters. In this and the following chapters on web applications, our toolchain will consist of services from AWS:

- AWS API Gateway as the HTTP proxy
- AWS Lambda for computing
- AWS S3 for static file serving
- AWS CloudFront for the CDN
- AWS RDS for RDBMS management
- **AWS Certificate Manager (ACM)** for free certificate management

While AWS is the dominant player in the Platform as a service (PaaS) ecosystem, it is by no means the only choice. While reading this chapter and others in this book, remember that the patterns presented should apply to any cloud provider, albeit sometimes with a certain degree of adaptation.

You may be questioning the reasoning behind discussing other services such as S3 and RDS. Very often, perhaps usually, when people say *serverless* they are talking about functions as a service with AWS Lambda, or equivalent services from different cloud providers. This question is a valid one, but it's also critical to remember that our definition for serverless architectures in this book is complete systems where you don't need to manage any operating systems yourself. Your goal is not to maintain a single real or virtual server and push the hard work to your favorite cloud provider, allowing you to focus on your application. Admittedly, not all cloud providers have the vast number of services at our disposal as in the AWS ecosystem. Take this into consideration when choosing a PaaS upon which to build your serverless applications.

Building a system with a Function as a service (FaaS) backbone for the business logic is a step in the right direction; however, if you are still managing a database, are you serverless? Managing your own RDBMS or web server for the serving of static assets puts you outside of the serverless architecture box, even if your compute layer is serverless.

In `Chapter 1`, *Introduction*, I listed a few of the popular frameworks that allow us to manage, deploy, and maintain serverless applications. All of our sample applications in this book will use the Serverless Framework (`https://serverless.com/`), which will help us glue various services and systems together, allow us to deploy code, and provide much more functionality to make the development process faster and more straightforward. Just as with cloud providers, you have multiple choices for frameworks and utilities. Covering all of the options is outside the scope of this book and, for simplicity, we will stick with the Serverless Framework, which is mature, well used, and frequently updated.

 From this point on, I will refer to the Serverless Framework when talking about the framework itself to differentiate it from the general serverless topic. Due to the name *Serverless*, the Serverless Framework can be a bit confusing in the context of a book about serverless design patterns. From here on, simply be on the lookout for the Serverless Framework if we're discussing details of how to deploy, manage, or otherwise control resources on our cloud provider, AWS.

Our example project will be a REST API for professional coffee evaluation, called cupping in the coffee realm. Coffee cupping at its core is nothing more than a fancy spreadsheet of scores for individual coffees, where scores are applied to one or more criteria, such as acidity, body, uniformity, and so on. If you enjoy coffee and APIs as I do, you should enjoy this and subsequent chapters.

System architecture

At first glance, a three-tier web application using a REST API can be an easy topic and pattern. After all, there are only three layers, which are responsible for very discrete tasks, and the final result is just a web application after all. However, there are many nuances and areas for tweaking with any web application. Serverless web applications are no different. This chapter will attempt to cover as many areas as possible, but it's impossible to include every possible configuration or design option.

Seeing as we are responsible software designers, let's sketch out our architecture at a high level and drill down into more detail as we work through the different layers:

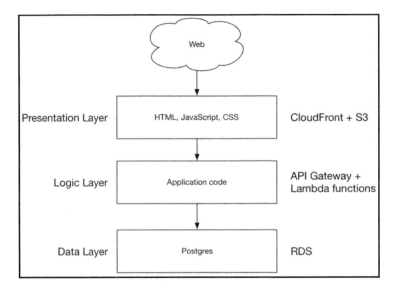

This diagram should look familiar as it's the backbone of many client-server web applications out there today. Let's walk through the different layers, going from the top down. After discussing these layers at a high level, we'll get into the implementation details with a real-world example.

You can find all of the code in this chapter in the following repository:

```
https://github.com/brianz/serverless-design-patterns/tree/master/ch2
```

 Even though a common and arguably simple pattern, there are many possible complexities when deploying a stack like this on AWS with a serverless architecture. While AWS is the PaaS of choice for this and subsequent chapters, there are many topics that cannot be covered in great depth due to the size of AWS as a topic by itself. If you get stuck or are confused by any missing content, feel free to open a GitHub issue at the preceding repository to begin a dialog and I'll do my best to help.

Presentation layer

Static files may be served from numerous places. In our case, we will use two different AWS services which will provide respectable performance shipping assets down to the client, as well as fault tolerance and caching, among other things. Our HTML, CSS, and JavaScript files will all live in an S3 bucket. We will then create a CDN using CloudFront, AWS's CDN offering. CloudFront will not only give us better performance than S3 by itself; we will gain the ability to globally distribute and cache our content, in addition to serving files from our very own custom domain using a free TLS certificate from AWS Certificate Manager.

Logic layer

The logical layer is the guts of our application, our code. In this and other examples, we'll use Python as our programming language and deploy our functions as isolated compute units in AWS Lambda. The Serverless Framework will make this quite painless, and this will be the foundation for moving fast and iterating on our code.

Data layer

While not the core focus of this book, running databases is an integral part of modern-day web applications. In this pattern, we'll use a hosted PostgreSQL, which the AWS **Relational Data Store (RDS)** service will manage for us.

Logic layer

Application code is likely the area of most interest and the layer that has the most changes from a traditional web application hosted on a managed server, so let's start with that.

Application code and function layout

Let's differentiate two classifications of our organization for the logical layer:

- Organization of the Lambda functions themselves, within AWS
- Organization of the application code

Lambda functions are the unit of work in Lambda and other FaaS providers (for simplicity and clarity, I will refer to these as Lambda functions from here on out). A single Lambda function may be updated or deployed in isolation without affecting other Lambda functions.

Organization of the Lambda functions

With a REST API, there are a few options you have as to how each API endpoint maps to a function. The primary options in this design are whether to have a single Lambda function handle a single HTTP verb/resource combination, or whether to have a single lambda function handle all HTTP verbs for a particular resource. It should become more evident as we work through this chapter that Lambda function organization and application code organization are related, but not the same:

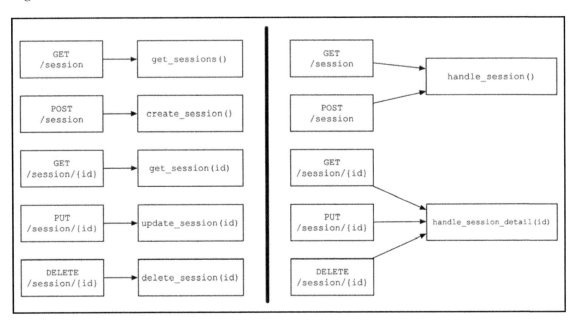

In the preceding diagram, we see a possible Lambda function layout for a REST API. On the left, unique functions handle a unique CRUD event and resource combination. On the right, Lambda functions perform actions on a single resource but with different actions (create, read, update, or delete).With the first model (left side of the diagram), each REST endpoint is mapped to a single Lambda function. This design provides fine-grained control for updating functions, allowing for the deployment of a single API endpoint without the danger of inadvertently affecting other APIs.

The major downside is that this may quickly become unwieldy as the API grows. Imagine the case of an API with 20 resources (`session`, `user`, and so on), each with three to four actions / HTTP verbs. If you follow this scenario through with some basic multiplication, the quick growth of the Lambda functions that you'll need to manage and navigate will become obvious.

With the next design, logical groups of REST endpoints are grouped and triggered, in effect the main function that routes the request to the appropriate handler. If you imagine the simple case of listing `sessions` from this API, an HTTP `GET` would come into the `/session` endpoint, which would trigger the `handle_sessions()` function. As a part of this payload, our application code would know that a `GET` method was invoked and would then invoke a `get_sessions()` function, perhaps the same as in the previous design. The significant benefit of this architecture is that the number of Lambda functions is drastically reduced over the previous design. The downside is that deploying updates affects all REST endpoints, which are handled by a single function. However, this may also be a benefit. If there were a bug in some shared code that affected all `/session/{id}` endpoints (`GET`, `PUT`, and `DELETE`), we'd only need to update a single function to fix them all. With the previous design, we would need to update three functions individually.

For this chapter, we will use the grouped design so that we have a single Lambda function for groups of REST endpoints. Each group will share a common URL pattern, and the HTTP verb will be used to trigger different functions within the application code.

Organization of the application code

Organization of our application code is entirely different than our prior discussion, although there is a bit of overlap.

Laying out application code in a serverless project is slightly different than in a traditional web application. While the differences aren't that drastic, I find serverless projects a bit more susceptible and intolerant of designs or layouts that are not thought through in detail. Because it's so easy to get started, it's also easy to start moving in the wrong direction before thinking through and answering essential design decisions.

Over the years, these are a few of the big lessons I've learned when writing serverless application code:

- Configuration should be done with environment variables, rather than different configuration files
- Application code should be well structured, highly modular, and namespaced
- Think through how many functions you need before coding begins

Configuration with environment variables

If you're familiar with the Twelve-Factor App or have worked with Docker much, you'll know that configuration may be done using environment variables rather than managing multiple disparate configuration files. According to The Twelve-Factor App (`https://12factor.net/config`):

> *"Env vars are easy to change between deploys without changing any code; unlike config files, there is little chance of them being checked into the code repo accidentally; and unlike custom config files, or other config mechanisms such as Java System Properties, they are a language- and OS-agnostic standard."*

Using environment variables for FaaS enables code deployments to different systems (dev, QA, production, and so on). Changing configuration can be as simple as updating a variable in your function's config. However, for safety and repeatability, environment variable changes should go through some process such as CI/CD to minimize the chance of errors.

On the flip side, if using file-based configuration, updating the application typically requires updating a file, possibly checking into source control and redeploying the entire application.

In my opinion, there is an enormous increase in productivity using environment variables when creating new systems or deploying between different systems. To perform a new stack deployment or update of an existing stack, you merely load up new environment variables and executes a standard set of steps that don't change between stacks. Due to the ease and speed with which you can do this, it encourages separation of stacks for different purposes (development, testing, production, and much more).

Code structure

With any new application, there are many ways to organize code on disk. The following structure has worked very well for my colleagues and me across multiple projects. I encourage readers to use this as a starting point and adapt as needed. If using Node.js or another supported language for your FaaS provider, this may look slightly different. Throughout this chapter, we will fill in our example coffee `cupping` API and will add more files as we build the application:

```
├── Makefile
├── README.md
├── envs/
│   ├── dev
│   ├── qa
```

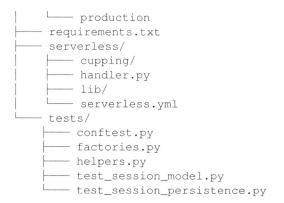

```
|     └── production
├── requirements.txt
├── serverless/
|     ├── cupping/
|     ├── handler.py
|     ├── lib/
|     └── serverless.yml
└── tests/
      ├── conftest.py
      ├── factories.py
      ├── helpers.py
      ├── test_session_model.py
      └── test_session_persistence.py
```

A `Makefile` may be something you skip. I use Docker as a host for application development since it's a reasonably easy way to manage environment variables during deployment and testing. A simple `Makefile` can make tedious tasks much less verbose by hiding the complexity behind a make target.

> For details on this Docker methodology, I'll point you to a detailed blog post at `http://blog.brianz.bz/post/structuring-serverless-applications-with-python/`. It'd be perfectly acceptable to run your serverless application development on your primary computer without any extra virtualization (Docker, VirtualBox, and so on). This Docker/Makefile pattern has worked quite well for me recently across multiple projects. I still edit files using my host system, but all runtime work (testing, deployment, building packages, and so on) is done from within a Docker container.

The `envs` directory holds environment variable files, which are simple `key=value` pairs. Each environment has a corresponding file of the same name. Looking at preceding the example, it should be clear where the configuration resides for each environment and what you'd need to do when creating a new environment.

We place all the code into the `serverless` directory, including application code we write, as well as its dependencies. Our application code is namespaced into the `cupping` directory. We will install third-party libraries into `lib`. Of course, as you write your application, your application code will be namespaced to something that is appropriate for your project. I recommend using a meaningful name rather than something generic such as `code` or `app`, just to aid new developers who come after you in navigating the source tree and for general clarity and explicitness.

Alongside the application code live two files—`serverless.yml`, which defines and controls the Serverless Framework, and `handler.py`, which is the main entry point for any API calls. In the preceding diagram, we discussed how logical groupings of API endpoints would be handled by a common function within a given file, `handler.py`, which will be the entry point for these API calls and delegate the hard to work to other functions. In some ways, `handler.py` has a straightforward job, which will become apparent.

As responsible developers, we will make sure our code is well tested. With `pytest` as our testing framework of choice in this project, all unit test files live in a single `test` folder with some additional helpers and configuration utilities. In the preceding example, there are only two test files; more will be added to the final project. Your exact testing strategy isn't as important as the simple fact of having well-written tests. Serverless projects are incredibly fast to deploy, and there may be an inclination to forego tests. Why write unit tests when you can just deploy it for real and test it manually? One cannot overstate the benefit of having robust unit tests. Regardless of your tooling or language, all serverless projects of any decent size or complexity will benefit from tests, which you may run locally or on a continuous integration platform or system. Tests give us the confidence to deploy quickly and often and also set us up for continuous delivery moving forward, allowing a CD system to deploy our code automatically only after our tests have passed.

Function layout

In our example, we will implement a pattern where a single Lambda function will handle a single grouping of URL endpoints. The initial set of endpoints that we will implement will be the following:

- List coffee cupping sessions: GET /session
- Create a coffee cupping session: POST /session
- Get coffee cupping session details: GET /session/{id}
- Delete a coffee cupping session: DELETE /session/{id}

Two unique URLs will map to two Lambda functions. These lambda functions will be responsible for inspecting the HTTP request passed in from API Gateway, determining what HTTP method is being called, and invoking the appropriate application code to fulfill the request:

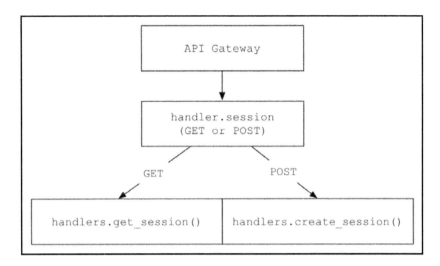

Request routing for a /session endpoint. The application code will inspect the HTTP method and route to the appropriate application code for execution.

Presentation layer

Presentation layers are not necessarily the most exciting area but, in reality, they are the entry point for your entire web application, and you should think through the details carefully. Naive deployments of HTML, CSS, and JavaScript files may result in slow load times, which has a noticeable impact on user experience.

When building serverless systems on top of AWS, there are a few different services that enable us to host static assets quite easily. Other PaaS systems have similar offerings, although there may not be a one-to-one comparison with all of the AWS services.

File storage with S3

Any frontend assets need a filesystem as a home. In this case, the natural choice is AWS **Simple Storage Service (S3)**, which is Amazon's high durability object storage service. S3 advertises 99.999999999% durability, so it's safe to say our files will be available when we need them. While it's possible to serve content from S3 as a website on a custom domain, it's not the best choice for this scenario. AWS CloudFront will aid us in distributing files to end users quickly and efficiently.

CDN with CloudFront

CloudFront is Amazon's CDN service. A CDN's primary focus is to improve the delivery of static assets to the end user. This task is typically accomplished by running multiple **points of presence (POPs)** around the globe and distributing your contents in those various geographic locations. When a user somewhere on the planet requests one or more of your files, the CDN can fetch the content that is closest to the user to minimize latency. Of course, this is only one small and dumbed-down explanation of a single CDN feature. The bottom line is that CDNs help us to speed up delivery of our content and should be used in any web application.

CloudFront has some very nice features that will allow us to integrate with other AWS services. We will create a CloudFront distribution that will pull our content from S3. In this way, CloudFront is a layer that aids in the acceleration of content delivery but does not own any content itself. We'll be able to configure caching controls to suit our needs and will also be able to serve our content over a custom domain with a free TLS certificate from AWS Certificate Manager. All of this is possible thanks to CloudFront.

Data layer

It's safe to say that most web applications today have some data store, whether it's a relational database (PostgreSQL, MySQL, SQLServer, and so on), a non-relational database (MongoDB, Redis, Cassandra, and so on), or even static file storage (S3, OS filesystem, and so on).

AWS RDS service will manage a PostgreSQL database for our coffee `cupping` application. RDS offers different RDBMS choices, most notably PostgreSQL, MySQL, Oracle, and SQLServer. There are other choices, and I encourage you to take a look at the various offerings. For this exercise, we'll be using a standard PostgreSQL database hosted on RDS. Many configuration options come with RDS, which we won't cover. Just know that it's possible and quite simple to run, configure, and manage a high-availability RDBMS instance using RDS. Other PaaS providers offer similar services for relational databases.

Writing our logic layer

Since we've covered the overall design and different layers, let's get down to the implementation of our application code.

Application entrypoint

Every application, web or otherwise, needs a primary entry point. In our case, we'll use `handler.py` to begin application execution when a Lambda function is invoked. Serverless Framework applications will generate a `handler.py` file when you bootstrap a new project, so this pattern should be familiar to anyone who has used Serverless before. If you've never worked with the Serverless Framework, what follows will be a thorough introduction:

```python
import sys

from pathlib import Path

# Munge our sys path so libs can be found
CWD = Path(__file__).resolve().cwd() / 'lib'
sys.path.insert(0, str(CWD))

import simplejson as json

from cupping.handlers.session import (
        handle_session,
        handle_session_detail,
)

from cupping.exceptions import Http404

CORS_HEADERS = {
        'Access-Control-Allow-Origin': '*',
        'Access-Control-Allow-Credentials': True
}

def session(event, context):
    """/session endpoint for POST or GET"""
    http_method = event['httpMethod']

    status_code = 200
    response = {}

    try:
        response = handle_session(http_method, event)
    except Exception as e:
        status_code = 500
        # TODO - log error
        response = {'errors': ['Unexpected server error']}

    response = {
        'statusCode': status_code,
```

```
            'body': json.dumps(response),
            'headers': CORS_HEADERS,
        }

        return response


    def session_detail(event, context):
        http_method = event['httpMethod']

        status_code = 200
        response = {}

        try:
            response = handle_session_detail(http_method, event)
        except Http404 as e:
            status_code = 404
            response = {'errors': [str(e)]}
        except Exception as e:
            status_code = 500
            # TODO - log error
            response = {'errors': ['Unexpected server error']}

        response = {
            'statusCode': status_code,
            'body': json.dumps(response),
            'headers': CORS_HEADERS,
        }

        return response
```

Our `handler.py` code isn't very complicated and delegates most application logic to different parts of our application code (namespaced into the `cupping` package). This pattern of having a single entry point for all Lambda functions is advantageous for a few reasons.

When Lambda functions execute, they only know what they know. That is, we as application developers are used to installing extra packages in some known location (which is the default system package location) or perhaps creating a Python `virtualenv` and configuring our server to look there during the import cycle. During a Lambda, we are responsible for managing this ourselves. Application code has no idea where to look for packages beyond the built-in libraries without being told where to look. The code block below shows how to manipulate Python's `path` so that it can find any extra packages we wish to use.

```
    import sys
```

```python
from pathlib import Path

# Munge our sys path so libs can be found
CWD = Path(__file__).resolve().cwd() / 'lib'
sys.path.insert(0, str(CWD))
```

These four lines of code accomplish the task of resolving the current directory of our `handler.py` file and appending a `/lib` onto it. The result is the absolute path of the `lib` directory where we've installed all of our system packages. During the deployment step, the Serverless Framework will package all directories and files that reside at or below the same directory level as the `serverless.yml` file, resulting in our `lib` being available to our application code during runtime. Any import statement for a third-party library will work as expected, only after the addition of the full path to `lib` being manually added to the system path. In the preceding example, there is an import for the third-party `simplejson` module. Had this import been placed above the `sys.path.insert` call, it would have failed.

When this path manipulation occurs as soon as possible (that is, as soon as `handler.py` is invoked), other parts of our application code can import packages without the danger of the import failing. If this path manipulation is done across different files only when a particular package is needed, errors will be inevitable as you will at some point forget to include this logic. Additionally, doing this work in a single place means there is no duplication of logic.

Application logic

Since our handler function is so simple, let's take a look at the application code to see what exactly is going on. Our coffee cupping API is fairly simple and only handles a single resource type at this point, a coffee `cupping` session object. Before moving forward, it's helpful to take a look at the shape of this resource type:

```json
{
  "name": "Cupping session for Serverless Patterns",
  "formName": "Modified SCAA",
  "cuppings": [
  {
    "name": "Guatemala Huehuetenango",
    "overallScore": "85.5",
    "scores": {
      "Aroma": 8.6,
      "Body": 8,
      "Flavor": 10
    },
    "notes": "This was pretty good",
```

```
      "descriptors": ["woody", "berries"]
    },
    {
      "name": "Ethiopia Yirgacheffe",
      "overallScore": "90",
      "scores": {
        "Aroma": 8.6,
        "Body": 8,
        "Flavor": 10
      },
      "notes": "Nice",
      "descriptors": ["blueberry"]
    }
  ]
}
```

Much of the logic of this application is simply the transformation back and forth between JSON and database records. The actual application code isn't that important in the context of this book. If you'd like to learn more about the actual implementation, I encourage you to view the source code at https://github.com/brianz/serverless-design-patterns.

The logic in handler.py will delegate the API requests to the cupping/handlers/session.py file, which you can see in the following code. The purpose here is to service requests for a particular URL pattern (which is /session, /session/{id}) and particular HTTP verb (that is, GET, POST, DELETE) and execute the appropriate application code:

```python
from schematics.exceptions import DataError

from .decorators import decode_json
from .helpers import (
        create_session_from_json_payload,
        prettify_schematics_errors,
)

from ..models import (
        CuppingModel,
        SessionModel,
)
from ..persistence import Session, queries
from ..exceptions import Http404, InvalidInputData


def get_sessions(data):
    sessions = queries.get_sessions()
    models = [SessionModel.from_row(s) for s in queries.get_sessions()]
```

```python
    return {'sessions': [m.to_native() for m in models]}


@decode_json
def create_session(json_payload):
    if not json_payload or not hasattr(json_payload, 'get'):
        return {'errors': ['Invalid input data']}

    print('Creating session', json_payload)

    try:
        session = create_session_from_json_payload(json_payload)
        print('Created session: %s' % (session.id, ))
        response = {
                'session': {
                    'id': session.id,
                    'name': session.name,
                }
        }
    except InvalidInputData as e:
        response = {'errors': e.errors}

    return response


def _get_session_from_path_parameters(data):
    try:
        session_id = int(data.get('pathParameters', {}).get('id'))
    except (AttributeError, TypeError, ValueError):
        raise Http404('Invalid session id')

    session = queries.get_session_by_id(session_id)
    if session is None:
        raise Http404('Invalid session id')

    return session


def get_session(data):
    print('Reading session', data)
    session = _get_session_from_path_parameters(data)
    model = SessionModel.from_row(session)
    return {'session': model.to_native()}


def handle_session(http_method, payload):
    method_map = {
            'GET': get_sessions,
```

```
                'POST': create_session,
        }
        method = http_method.upper()
        return method_map[method](payload)


    def handle_session_detail(http_method, payload):
        method_map = {
                'GET': get_session,
                'DELETE': delete_session,
        }
        method = http_method.upper()
        return method_map[method](payload)
```

The final two functions are the gateway into this part of our application, where HTTP verbs are mapped to different functions.

Wiring handler.py to Lambda via API Gateway

Next, we need to wire up our API endpoints to Lambda and our `handler.py` entry point. This wiring looks like this in a `serverless.yml` configuration file:

```
functions:
  HandleSession:
    handler: handler.session
    events:
      - http:
          path: session
          method: get
          cors: true
      - http:
          path: session
          method: post
          cors: true
  HandleSessionDetail:
    handler: handler.session_detail
    events:
      - http:
          path: session/{id}
          method: get
          cors: true
          request:
            parameters:
              paths:
                id: true
      - http:
```

```
path: session/{id}
method: delete
cors: true
request:
  parameters:
    paths:
      id: true
```

We define two Lambda functions that have different configuration options, `HandleSession` and `HandleSessionDetail`.

Under each function's name, there are multiple statements that control configuration. Look at both sections and you'll notice the `handler:` statement, which instructs Lambda what code to call when the Lambda function is executed. For both, we'll be running one of the Python functions in `handler.py` that we covered in the preceding code snippet.

But what calls these Lambda functions in the first place? The `events:` section is responsible for setting up invocation points and making the connection between a particular event and our Lambda function. Across the FaaS landscape, functions are invoked in response to an event. In the AWS landscape, the number of events that can trigger a Lambda function is quite large. In this scenario, we are configuring events to be HTTP endpoints with a particular path and HTTP method. API Gateway is the proxy that will provide us with unique HTTPS URLs, which get wired up to our Lambda functions according to our configuration. As you read through the configuration, our design and intent should be apparent. Again, there are a seemingly infinite number of ways to set up an API with these technologies and this example just scratches the surface to discuss the overall pattern.

 Because the frontend JavaScript code will be making HTTP requests to the serverless backend, which is hosted on a different domain, CORS will need to be set up for each API endpoint. Controlling CORS is simple to do by adding `cors: true` for each endpoint in `serverless.yml`. In addition to this setting, the application code will explicitly need to return the proper headers in the responses.

Deploying the REST API

Now the fun part, we'll deploy our REST API using the Serverless Framework. At this point, we have not discussed the various configuration options when implementing serverless architectures on AWS. I'll cover different possibilities, and our particular configuration, later on in this chapter.

My pattern of using Docker as a build and deployment tool makes this process a bit easier. You are not required to do this, and there are likely other ways to make the process even simpler.

We will do all package building and deployment from inside a running Docker container, which I start and enter with the following `Makefile` target:

```
brianz@gold(master=)$ ENV=dev make shell
```

This equates to the following Docker command:

```
docker run --rm -it \
        -v `pwd`:/code \
        --env ENV=$(ENV) \
        --env-file envs/$2 \
        --name=coffee-cupping-$(ENV) \
        verypossible/serverless:1.20.0-python3 bash
```

There is nothing magical here. We're starting up a Docker container from an image that contains the Serverless Framework as well as some other Python packages for a Python 3 runtime. The main trick is that, based on the ENV setting upon creation of the container, we pull environment variables from the desired `envs` files and load them into the running container. Those environment variables can then be referenced from within `serverless.yml` and injected into the Lambda functions, hence controlling configuration of the final application by starting from files on our local system. Full details are out of scope, but can be reviewed at `http://blog.brianz.bz/post/structuring-serverless-applications-with-python/`.

 The `Makefile` and commands I'm running here are not very sophisticated; however, they may appear to be so if you are unfamiliar with Docker or make. I encourage those unfamiliar with them to read through the `Makefile` targets and do a bit of exploration on their own at `https://github.com/brianz/serverless-design-patterns/blob/master/ch2/Makefile`. Feel free to open a GitHub issue if you get stuck or need more clarity.

Now that we're inside a container with all of our configuration set from environment variables, we can deploy the entire stack. Our first step is to ensure we have our libraries built and installed into the `lib` directory. In the Python world, the `pip` command can help us. Take a look at the `Makefile` in the repository for details. Our steps for doing the initial deployment are, therefore, as follows:

```
root@091655eda5d0:/code# make libs
......
```

```
# packages now installed in libs
....
root@091655eda5d0:/code# make deploy
cd serverless && sls deploy -s dev
Serverless: Packaging service...
Serverless: Excluding development dependencies...
Serverless: Uploading CloudFormation file to S3...
Serverless: Uploading artifacts...
Serverless: Uploading service .zip file to S3 (5.27 MB)...
Serverless: Validating template...
Serverless: Updating Stack...
Serverless: Checking Stack update progress...
.............
Serverless: Stack update finished...
Service Information
service: coffee-cupping
stage: dev
region: us-west-2
api keys:
 None
endpoints:
 GET -
https://2treukfv8j.execute-api.us-west-2.amazonaws.com/dev/session
 POST -
https://2treukfv8j.execute-api.us-west-2.amazonaws.com/dev/session
 GET -
https://2treukfv8j.execute-api.us-west-2.amazonaws.com/dev/session/{id}
 DELETE -
https://2treukfv8j.execute-api.us-west-2.amazonaws.com/dev/session/{id}
functions:
 HandleSession: coffee-cupping-dev-HandleSession
```

Deploying the Postgres database

Many frameworks for working with AWS serverless architectures expose access to
CloudFormation, AWS's tool for managing multiple related resources as a single entity.
The Serverless Framework is no different and, in fact, the CloudFormation interface is
verbatim CloudFormation templating with a few nice add-ons specifically for variables,
environment variables included. A common theme here is that this is a huge topic and the
details are out of the scope of this book.

`CloudFormation` creates the RDS instance on our behalf with several lines of setup in `serverless.yml`. Details aside, note how there are multiple references to `${env:VPC_ID}` and other calls to `${env:}`. The `${env}` syntax is a method for pulling variables from the environment that exists in the Docker container from our process of starting up the container. You may accomplish the same thing on your host system provided you have a way of managing environment variables.

Much of the complexity of this setup comes from the fact that Lambda functions by default will not have network access to AWS resources inside a **virtual private cloud** (**VPC**). Since RDS instances need to run inside a VPC, the Lambda functions need to be configured to run inside the same VPC and permissions set up accordingly:

```
resources:
  Resources:
    ServerlessSecurityGroup:
      Type: AWS::EC2::SecurityGroup
      Properties:
        GroupDescription: SecurityGroup for Serverless Functions
        VpcId: ${env:VPC_ID}
    RDSSecurityGroup:
      Type: AWS::EC2::SecurityGroup
      Properties:
        GroupDescription: Ingress for RDS Instance
        VpcId: ${env:VPC_ID}
        SecurityGroupIngress:
        - IpProtocol: tcp
          FromPort: '5432'
          ToPort: '5432'
          SourceSecurityGroupId:
            Ref: ServerlessSecurityGroup
    RDSSubnetGroup:
      Type: AWS::RDS::DBSubnetGroup
      Properties:
        DBSubnetGroupDescription: RDS Subnet Group
        SubnetIds:
          - ${env:SUBNET_ID_A}
          - ${env:SUBNET_ID_B}
          - ${env:SUBNET_ID_C}
    RDSPostgresInstance:
      Type: AWS::RDS::DBInstance
      Properties:
        AllocatedStorage: 100
        AutoMinorVersionUpgrade: true
        AvailabilityZone: ${self:provider.region}a
        DBInstanceClass: db.t2.micro
        DBName: ${env:CUPPING_DB_NAME}
```

```
DBSubnetGroupName:
  Ref: RDSSubnetGroup
Engine: postgres
EngineVersion: 9.6.2
MasterUsername: ${env:CUPPING_DB_USERNAME}
MasterUserPassword: ${env:CUPPING_DB_PASSWORD}
PubliclyAccessible: false
VPCSecurityGroups:
  - Fn::GetAtt: RDSSecurityGroup.GroupId
```

During deployment, the Serverless Framework will add any defined Resources into the default CloudFormation template and deploy them together. Having our database described, we can perform a make deploy and see our dedicated PostgreSQL resource.

 RDS and other hosted data stores are not silver bullets. These systems can still go down, and there are real constraints concerning computing power. However, a significant benefit of using a hosted data store is the hard work of managing, monitoring, and configuring is delegated to someone else. Serverless is not accurate in this case for a variety of reasons. I will assert that a hosted database eases much of the burden of managing your system and is an excellent fit in a truly serverless architecture.

Setting up static assets

Setting up an S3 bucket and CloudFront distribution to host static media isn't complicated and, in theory, we could add this to the Resources section of our serverless.yml file. The ability of Serverless to manage so many resources via CloudFormation is a slippery slope, since setting up systems can quickly become an exercise in learning and debugging CloudFormation. Another downside of a growing Resources section in the serverless.yml file is that deployments will take longer and longer. It's possible to only deploy application code during development, which results in single-digit second deployments; but when some system resource is updated, including environment variables, the entire CloudFormation stack needs to updated.

Rather than creating the S3 bucket and CloudFront distribution via serverless.yml, we can use a separate CloudFormation template designed just for this purpose. Another reason for splitting this out into a separate step is that this layer rarely changes. Once the CloudFront distribution is set up, there is a good chance you won't need to change anything for a very long time, if ever.

The following repository contains a `CloudFormation` template, a helper script, and documentation to set up a single - page web application on AWS:

`https://github.com/verypossible/cloudfront-single-page-app`

Again, you may read the details of this stack creation in the GitHub repository. After we choose one this stack with the necessary variables, we will end up with the following:

- An S3 bucket, which will host all of our static content
- A CloudFront distribution, which will pull and cache content from S3
- A free TLS certificate for `*.cupperslog.com`
- A Route53 record, which does the following:
  - Points `https://cupperslog.com` to the CloudFront distribution
  - Redirects any `http://` traffic to `https://`
  - Caches static assets for 10 minutes:

```
brianz@gold(master=)$ AWS_DEFAULT_REGION=us-east-1 ./manage-
stack.sh create --domain cupperslog.com --zone-id ZNGYF5FXIUL0Z --
name cupperslog
{
    "StackId": "arn:aws:cloudformation:us-
east-1:875406499000:stack/cupperslog/e7f15a50-
b03c-11e7-97b0-5001ff34b4a6"
}
```

CloudFront distributions can take from several minutes to a couple of hours to be created, which is another good reason that we're doing this separate from our application code and database. Once finished, all that is required is uploading static assets to the S3 bucket that `CloudFormation` created for you. Ensure that the access control policy is set to `public-read` since this is a publicly accessible website. Uploading is accomplished via many tools, the AWS CLI tool being one of them:

```
brianz@gold$ aws s3 cp \
    build/ \
    --acl public-read \
    --recurisve \
    s3://cupperslog-s3bucketforstaticcontent-nswgo5ega4r1
```

 Other tools I've used for S3 file management are Cyberduck for OS X, S3 Organizer for Firefox, and the regular AWS web interface. They all do more or less the same thing, so pick what works for you.

For our example application, the frontend will consist of a simple React application that allows users to do the following:

- List coffee `cupping` sessions
- View coffee `cupping` session details
- Create a new coffee `cupping` session
- Delete a coffee `cupping` session

It should be clear that there is no authentication and no notion of a user in these examples. This application was built to demonstrate a serverless pattern, and even critical details such as user authentication and authorization wouldn't fit in this single chapter.

Viewing the deployed web application

With everything in place, we can now upload our frontend assets to S3. We won't review the actual frontend React code, but if you're curious, you can take a look at that UI code in the GitHub repository at `https://github.com/brianz/serverless-design-patterns/tree/master/ch2/ui`.

Using the preceding `aws s3 cp` command, a final production build of the frontend code is uploaded to S3 and ultimately serves the content as requested by the CloudFront CDN. When the first page is rendered, a request is made to our serverless backend to get a listing of all coffee `cupping` sessions:

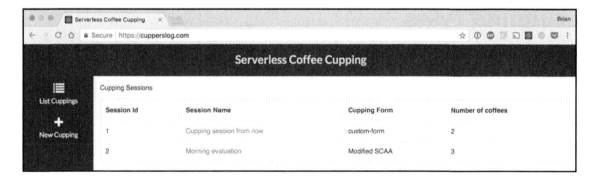

A very common issue, and one that people often forget about, is cross-origin resource sharing, which is a security measure put in place by browsers. Our serverless backend was set up to sidestep this issue, making development much quicker. For a real production system, it's best to only allow CORS for your own domain or, better yet, run the serverless backend on your own domain rather than the autogenerated domain from API Gateway. Running the serverless API on your own custom domain is possible using AWS API Gateway, but this is out of the scope of this chapter.

Clicking on a single row, the detail page for the particular session is loaded:

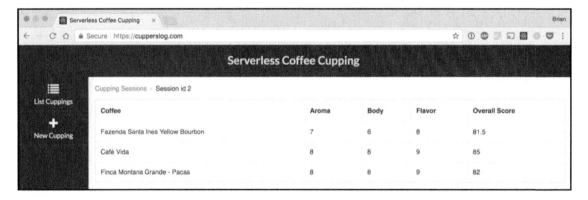

Running tests

Since we're responsible developers, we have written a full suite of unit tests for our application. For now, tests are run manually inside our Docker container. The Docker image used has `py.test` installed, as well as some coverage tools.

The only dependency to running tests is PostgreSQL. Docker again makes it very simple to run a PostgreSQL container and hook it up to our application container. Multiple strategies exist for this, from running Docker Compose to merely starting up a container with `docker run` and linking the containers manually. For simplicity, I use the latter option. See the targets in the repository `Makefile` for details.

To run tests, inside the container, we execute `make tests`. I have trimmed much of the output for brevity and clarity:

```
root@d8dd5cc4bb86:/code# make tests
py.test --cov=serverless/ --cov-report=html tests/
Connected to: postgresql://postgres:@cupping-rltest-
postgres:5432/test_cupping_log
........
==== test session starts ====
platform linux -- Python 3.6.2, pytest-3.2.1, py-1.4.34, pluggy-0.4.0
rootdir: /code, inifile:
plugins: mock-1.6.2, cov-2.5.1
collected 105 items

tests/test_cupping_model.py .........
tests/test_cupping_persistence.py ....................
tests/test_handler.py ...
tests/test_helpers.py .
tests/test_session_handler.py ..........................
tests/test_session_models.py ......
tests/test_session_persistence.py ...................................

--- coverage: platform linux, python 3.6.2-final-0 ---
Coverage HTML written to dir htmlcov

==== 105 passed in 2.04 seconds ===
```

The result is an `htmlcov/index.html` file that visually shows test coverage throughout the application and highlights lines that were not executed during the test run:

Coverage report: 92%

Module	statements	missing ↑	excluded	branches	partial	coverage
serverless/cupping/db/mixins.py	33	14	0	6	1	51%
serverless/cupping/handlers/session.py	43	4	0	4	0	91%
serverless/handler.py	32	3	4	2	1	88%
serverless/cupping/db/__init__.py	52	2	48	8	3	92%
serverless/cupping/__init__.py	0	0	0	0	0	100%
serverless/cupping/constants.py	11	0	0	0	0	100%
serverless/cupping/exceptions.py	5	0	0	0	0	100%
serverless/cupping/handlers/__init__.py	0	0	0	0	0	100%
serverless/cupping/handlers/decorators.py	9	0	0	0	0	100%
serverless/cupping/handlers/helpers.py	34	0	0	16	1	98%
serverless/cupping/helpers.py	3	0	0	0	0	100%
serverless/cupping/models/__init__.py	2	0	0	0	0	100%
serverless/cupping/models/cupping.py	20	0	0	4	0	100%
serverless/cupping/models/session.py	14	0	0	4	0	100%
serverless/cupping/persistence/__init__.py	2	0	0	0	0	100%
serverless/cupping/persistence/base.py	7	0	0	0	0	100%
serverless/cupping/persistence/cupping.py	48	0	0	14	0	100%
serverless/cupping/persistence/queries.py	6	0	0	0	0	100%
serverless/cupping/persistence/session.py	41	0	0	10	0	100%
Total	**362**	**23**	**52**	**68**	**6**	**92%**

coverage.py v4.4.1, created at 2017-10-14 19:01

The preceding image is a test coverage report from the `pytest` and coverage libraries

Coverage may also be displayed on the console if we ask for it specifically:

```
----------- coverage: platform linux, python 3.6.2-final-0 -----------
Name Stmts Miss Branch BrPart Cover
----------------------------------------------------------------------
-------
serverless/cupping/__init__.py 0 0 0 0 100%
serverless/cupping/constants.py 11 0 0 0 100%
serverless/cupping/db/__init__.py 52 2 8 3 92%
serverless/cupping/db/mixins.py 33 14 6 1 51%
serverless/cupping/exceptions.py 5 0 0 0 100%
serverless/cupping/handlers/__init__.py 0 0 0 0 100%
```

```
serverless/cupping/handlers/decorators.py 9 0 0 0 100%
serverless/cupping/handlers/helpers.py 34 0 16 1 98%
serverless/cupping/handlers/session.py 43 4 4 0 91%
serverless/cupping/helpers.py 3 0 0 0 100%
serverless/cupping/models/__init__.py 2 0 0 0 100%
serverless/cupping/models/cupping.py 20 0 4 0 100%
serverless/cupping/models/session.py 14 0 4 0 100%
serverless/cupping/persistence/__init__.py 2 0 0 0 100%
serverless/cupping/persistence/base.py 7 0 0 0 100%
serverless/cupping/persistence/cupping.py 48 0 14 0 100%
serverless/cupping/persistence/queries.py 6 0 0 0 100%
serverless/cupping/persistence/session.py 41 0 10 0 100%
serverless/handler.py 32 3 2 1 88%
---------------------------------------------------------------------
-------
TOTAL 362 23 68 6 92%
```

Iteration and deployment

Inevitably, there will be multiple deployments when developing an application such as this, and even once the first production version has shipped. Serverless speeds up this process dramatically, and once you experience the increased velocity, you may have a hard time going back to your old ways.

A deployment with the Serverless Framework consists of one command with a couple of variations.

Deploying the entire stack

To deploy everything in the `serverless.yml` file, the `deploy` command is used, specifying the `stage (-s)` variable (which defaults to `dev`):

```
# serverless deploy -s $ENV
```

 The `make deploy` target in use for this chapter's example executes this exact command.

When doing a full deployment like this, Serverless will upload your Lambda resources and execute the entire `CloudFormation` template. Even with a simple `CloudFormation` template, this can take several seconds. With bigger stacks, it can be even longer. It's unfortunate that some people believe this is the only method of deploying application code with this framework. To make application code deployments even faster, we can specify precisely which functions to deploy.

Deploying the application code

Once you are in the state of code iteration and redeployment, you'll want to make that loop as short as possible. To accomplish this, specifying the function name when doing the deployment step goes through the process of uploading your Lambda function, but skips the `CloudFormation` update. In my experience, this results in deployments that are typically low single-digit seconds:

```
# serverless deploy function -s $ENV -f $FUNCTION_NAME
```

I can hear you thinking, what about doing deployments to a production system that is serving live traffic? Behind the scenes, AWS Lambda is using container technology to respond to events. During a deployment, any Lambda invocations continue doing their jobs as instructed. At a certain point, a new Lambda function will complete its upload and configuration process. Only at that time will the new function begin serving traffic. In short, the tricky dance of draining active connections and handing off new connections to new application state is handled for you. This behavior should be a standard feature among other FaaS providers. Users of other platforms should verify this on their own.

The `Makefile` used in this chapter's example has a target which helps speed up the deployment process even more. `make deploy function=FunctionName` may be used to deploy a single Lambda function, where `FunctionName` should be a name listed in the `serverless.yml` file (for example, `make deploy function=HandleSesion`). This works by skipping the `CloudFormation` update and only packaging and uploading a single function. `CloudFormation` updates will take a few to many seconds, whereas a single function deployment or update is typically low single-digit.

Summary

In this chapter, we walked through the entire process of creating a three-tier web application with a serverless architecture consisting of a view layer, data layer, and application layer and which is powered by AWS Lambda. All services employed in the example web application are from AWS, and none require managing a virtual machine or operating system directly.

Readers should have a good understanding of the advantages of such a system and how to start the process of structuring their application using this pattern. I presented several helpers and shortcuts that should aid readers in speeding up their development.

In Chapter 3, *A Three-Tier Web Application Pattern with GraphQL*, we will work through a similar pattern by porting the example application from a RESTful interface to a GraphQL interface.

A Three-Tier Web Application Pattern with GraphQL 3

In Chapter 2, *A Three-Tier Web Application Using REST*, we walked through the entire process of authoring a REST API on top of a serverless system with accompanying hosted services for the data and presentation layers. Our serverless logic layer was implemented with AWS Lambda and API Gateway, which provide many advantages regarding deployment, iteration speed, and scalability. REST APIs are well understood among the web development community and a safe choice when building a new web-based API. However, emerging tools and protocols are taking shape and providing us with alternatives to REST. GraphQL is arguably one of the most popular alternatives to REST APIs lately, evidenced by AWS and other platforms releasing hosted GraphQL services. You don't need to look very deep to find the uptick in GraphQL's popularity.

In this chapter, we'll walk through the process of updating the three-tier example API to use a GraphQL interface rather than a REST interface. These changes will focus on only the logic layer, as the data layer will not change at all. We will learn how to set up and author a single GraphQL serverless endpoint as opposed to multiple endpoints as in the REST-based design.

In this chapter, we will look into and discuss the following:

- How to author a GraphQL API using AWS Lambda and Python
- The differences in function layout between GraphQL and REST serverless applications
- How to query our GraphQL endpoint as a client

Introduction to GraphQL

REST has been around for nearly 20 years and remains a popular choice for web APIs, both internal and public. As popular as REST is, it does have its flaws and is more of an idea as opposed to a specification. Anyone who has designed or worked with third-party APIs knows that there is often little overlap in implementation and design choices from one API to another. At best, this makes using or designing REST APIs challenging. When approaching a new REST API, there is always the work of exploring the various API endpoints, hunting for the data you'll need, understanding the different resource types and how they relate, and so on. Of course, when working with a new API, there will always be some level of investment and discovery to learn the data with which you'll be working.

Facebook designed GraphQL internally in 2012 and released it to the public in 2015. GraphQL is the new kid on the block and is picking up substantial traction as an alternative to REST. While the end goal is the same as REST (to get data from a client to the server), the implementation and mechanisms for doing so are drastically different. Perhaps most different from REST, GraphQL is an actual specification that client and server implementations can reference and agree on. In contrast, REST is a set of principles and ideas that are subject to interpretation. GraphQL defines a new query language and allows clients to ask for the data they need consistently. With REST, the addition, removal, or permutation of return values usually requires server-side code changes. With GraphQL, clients are able to define the structure of the return payload in an ad hoc fashion on a query-by-query basis. For clients, the boundaries in a REST API are the endpoints provided at a given point in time and their return values, whereas the limits in a GraphQL API are the full domain of the API.

 GraphQL is a big and complex topic. It's still relatively new, especially when comparing it to REST and other web technologies. Because GraphQL digests so many of the complexities of a web API, any conversation about GraphQL quickly becomes a discussion about the intricacies of GraphQL itself. In this chapter, I attempt to give just the right amount of detail on GraphQL to demonstrate the underlying serverless pattern. If you find yourself wanting a deeper understanding of GraphQL during reading or at the end of this chapter, I encourage you to read the many articles and blog posts that exist on this topic. The following introduction from Facebook is a great place to start: `https://reactjs.org/blog/2015/05/01/graphql-introduction.html`.

In short, clients working with a GraphQL API can fetch precisely the data they need, no more, no less. Over-fetching (getting more data than the client needs) and under-fetching (needing to make multiple API calls to get the data the client needs) issues disappear when working with GraphQL, which arguably was a significant driver in Facebook's design of GraphQL and provides many benefits for clients. Another exciting and powerful attribute of GraphQL is that it isn't an HTTP-only specification. While HTTP is currently the primary use case, GraphQL isn't tied directly to HTTP and may be used with other transport protocols.

System architecture

Our system architecture, at a high level, will be the same as in the REST API version of our sample application. Requests from the web will hit the CloudFront CDN, which is backed by S3. Our JavaScript code from the served-up HTML files will query the serverless API, which itself will communicate with the RDS-backed data layer:

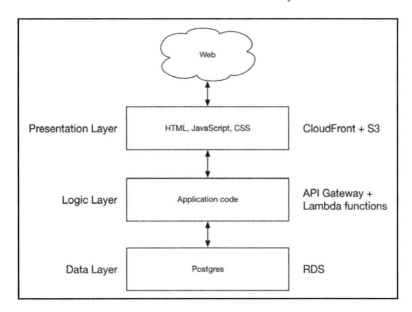

Thinking through this application from a top-down approach, the steps in fetching data will be the same regardless of how the logic layer is implemented:

- End-user requests a website
- Static assets are served to the user from CloudFront and S3

- Static assets request data via logic layer/web APIs (GraphQL in this case)
- Logic layer fetches/writes data from/to Postgres database in the data layer

Moving our example web application from a REST design to GraphQL means focusing on the **logic layer**, as the presentation and data layers won't change much, if at all. Of course, any changes to our API mean that our presentation layer (that is, the client) will need to change; however, as that is not our primary area of focus, we won't delve too deeply into the client-side changes.

You can find all of the code in this chapter in the following repository:

```
https://github.com/brianz/serverless-design-patterns/tree/master/ch3
```

Logic layer

GraphQL simplifies life for clients because there is a single HTTP endpoint. In some ways, this makes the pattern for a serverless GraphQL API extremely simple and in some ways quite dull.

If we were starting this GraphQL web application from scratch, there would be plenty of decisions to make and material to cover to make our application code modular, easy to test, and well designed. Since we're porting the example REST web application, we have already implemented the vast majority of the needed functionality and software layers. These sections may seem terser than expected, especially if you have skipped Chapter 2, *A Three-Tier Web Application using REST*. Any gaps in code organization or layout, configuration strategy, deployments, and so on can be filled by reviewing Chapter 2, *A Three-Tier Web Application using REST*.

Organization of the Lambda functions

REST APIs are built around resources that each own their own URI, in part to give clients a well-known or predictable way to interact. GraphQL takes a different approach. Note that the *QL* in GraphQL stands for *query language*. Data-fetching logic is moved into the query language itself, rather than being distributed among different API endpoints as in the case of REST. Clients no longer need to work through the process of the following:

- Determining what resource they need and where it lives on the list of URLs
- Looking up documentation to determine the input parameters and output data

- If applicable, reading the documentation on pagination or limiting of returned data

A formal specification currently found at `http://facebook.github.io/graphql/ October2016/` defines GraphQL in absolute terms. As with any specification, any framework or library that aims at providing GraphQL functionality to users must abide by this formal contract. Both clients and servers work within the bounds of this specification so that there is a single way to handle common bits of functionality. To keep these points in context, the logic for this functionality is implemented in a single endpoint and hence Lambda function, regardless of the resource or any other data being requested.

The following diagram shows what the move from a REST API to GraphQL looks like regarding supported URLs and backing functions:

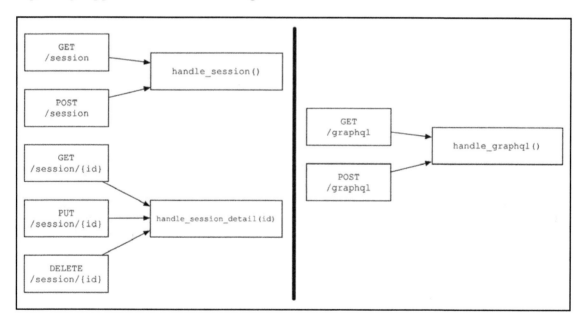

As we saw in `Chapter 2`, *A Three-Tier Web Application using REST,* a REST API in a serverless system is or may be composed of a serverless function (AWS Lambda or the like) for one or more API endpoints. As the API grows, so too does the number of serverless functions.

GraphQL, on the other hand, contains all of the logic for an entire API, including creation, reading, and updating of data. It should be clear from the preceding diagram that regardless of how a system changes, there are no changes required to the serverless functions backing the GraphQL API. Any changes in business logic or application logic are wrapped up in application code, in contrast to requiring changes in URL structure and hence serverless functions or layout.

For this chapter, we will be working on a single AWS Lambda function and HTTP endpoint that will handle all GraphQL requests. Do note, however, that GraphQL clients may make requests over both GET and POST, so our Lambda function will be set up to handle both request types.

 You can find more details on serving GraphQL over HTTP in the official documentation at http://graphql.org/learn/serving-over-http/.

Organization of the application code

As noted previously, organizing serverless functions and application code is not exactly the same thing. With a GraphQL system, our lives as developers are slightly more comfortable since there is only a single endpoint to support. The overall organization of application code isn't changing at all from our REST API. The only real changes are that there will be much *less* application code to manage, but the overall layout, structure, and routing strategy will not change in any way. For details, readers may review Chapter 2, *A Three-Tier Web Application using REST*.

Other parts of our API that will remain constant in the GraphQL implementation are the following:

- Configuration strategy via environment variables
- Overall code structure and layout

Function layout

Our GraphQL endpoint will be handled by a single AWS Lambda function, via either the
GET or POST HTTP method. For completeness, the diagram of the AWS API Gateway
request to the AWS Lambda function looks like the following:

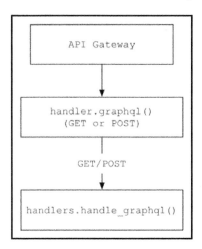

While it may seem a bit pedantic to review this, I think it's important to stress the simplicity
of this pattern and the advantages gained by adopting GraphQL. Of course, there are
always trade-offs, and GraphQL is no different. Since so much functionality is pushed
down into the logic layers, most of your time will likely be spent in application code,
ensuring your API provides the same functionality as before and learning the details of
GraphQL itself. Not being a GraphQL expert myself, and because GraphQL isn't
the main topic of this book, we won't be covering all of the possible scenarios and
functionality of a GraphQL API.

Presentation layer

In Chapter 2, *A Three-Tier Web Application using REST*, our React application was making
API calls to our REST endpoints. This REST API that we built returns JSON, which our
frontend code easily digests and feeds into our React code for rendering UI elements.

With a change to a GraphQL-based API, our frontend code will need to change somewhat drastically for the data-fetching sections. GraphQL behaves very differently than REST, and there is no corollary between a REST endpoint, which returns a known set of data, and GraphQL. Each GraphQL query is unique in that the client is responsible for asking for a specific set of data.

We won't review the changes to the frontend code. At the time of writing, popular choices for GraphQL for the frontend are Apollo and Relay. Apollo comes out of the Meteor Development Group and Facebook is behind Relay. Both are open source and popular in the GraphQL community. There are many resources on both topics all over the internet and readers are encouraged to learn more on their own. For this chapter, we'll interact with our GraphQL backend using an API client.

Writing the logic layer

Adding this GraphQL endpoint will consist of the following:

- Adding a new entry point to handle the new Lambda function
- Passing the HTTP payload (which is a GraphQL query or mutation) to a function that will execute GraphQL code

Admittedly, GraphQL is new enough that libraries and the ecosystem are not entirely polished or rich with documentation, at least in my experience. Still, it's possible to make quick progress, and once the basics are solved, GraphQL by its nature enables a vast range of functionality.

Since the coffee cupping example application is implemented using Python, we will continue down that path and augment it with some additional libraries for GraphQL. At the time of writing, Graphene is the de facto library for working with GraphQL from Python. Along with the base library, there are several other libraries that make working with various data stores easier. Luckily for us, one of the add-on libraries is Graphene-SQLAlchemy, which will work with our own SQLAlchemy code.

 You can learn more about Graphene and its related integrations at `http://graphene-python.org`.

Implementing the entry point

With the addition of a new Lambda function that will respond to requests at the `/graphql` endpoint, we need one new entry in our existing `handler.py` file. For consistency with the other handlers in this file, the function will do the following:

- Extract the HTTP method and payload from the request
- Hand the HTTP method and payload to another function for processing
- Construct and return the final response to API Gateway:

```
def graphql(event, context):
http_method = event['httpMethod']

response = handle_graphql(http_method, event)
status_code = 200

response = {
  'statusCode': status_code,
  'body': json.dumps(response),
  'headers': CORS_HEADERS,
}

return response
```

There isn't much to do in this function and one can see that the bulk of the logic is in the `handle_graphql` function, which we import at the top of the file and that lives in `cupping/handlers/graphql.py`. Using this pattern is extremely helpful since all of our path setups has already been completed and other standard code, such as the `cors` headers, is complete.

Implementing GraphQL queries

With the boilerplate out of the way, it's time to focus on our actual GraphQL implementation. Many software layers that powered the REST API will also power the GraphQL API, specifically the model/validation layer and persistence/SQLAlchemy layer.

If you are new to GraphQL, know there are two types of operations, which GraphQL treats differently and which require slightly different code, at least when using Python and Graphene. Those two actions are queries and mutations, or reads and writes, respectively. In this section, we will cover queries. This code provides all of the functionality for every query interaction in our example API. Details of each part of this code will be discussed in later. The main entry point is this handler code is the `handle_graphql` function:

```python
import json
import graphene

from graphene_sqlalchemy import SQLAlchemyObjectType

from .decorators import decode_json

from ..models import SessionModel
from ..persistence.cupping import Cupping
from ..persistence.session import Session
from ..persistence.queries import (
        get_cuppings,
        get_sessions,
)


class CuppingObject(SQLAlchemyObjectType):
    class Meta:
        model = Cupping


class SessionObject(SQLAlchemyObjectType):
    class Meta:
        model = Session


class Query(graphene.ObjectType):
    sessions = graphene.List(SessionObject, id=graphene.Int(),
    account_id=graphene.Int())
    cuppings = graphene.List(CuppingObject, session_id=graphene.Int())

    def resolve_cuppings(self, info, **filters):
        return get_cuppings(**filters)

    def resolve_sessions(self, info, **filters):
        return get_sessions(**filters)


# Global schema which will handle queries and mutations
schema = graphene.Schema(
```

```
            query=Query,
            types=[CuppingObject, SessionObject],
    )


@decode_json
def _handle_graphql(payload):
    query = payload['query']
    variables = payload.get('variables', {})
    result = schema.execute(query, variable_values=variables)
    success = True if not result.errors else False
    return success, result


def handle_graphql(http_method, payload):
    success, result = _handle_graphql(payload)
    if not success:
        errors = []
        for e in result.errors:
            try:
                e = json.loads(e.message)
            except:
                e = str(e)
            errors.append(e)
        return {'errors': errors}
    return result.data
```

The preceding code implements the same functionality as our REST API's GET endpoints, getting a listing of all cupping sessions and individual cupping sessions. Following on from the top-level handler.py, the handle_graphql function accepts an HTTP method, which isn't even used, along with a JSON-encoded payload from the request. From there, it's handed off to a small helper function that decodes the JSON payload via a decorator we authored earlier. Some light error handling ensures that errors come back in the right format. This function ultimately returns a Python dictionary with either errors or the result of the GraphQL execution. Ultimately, this dictionary is JSON-encoded and returned to the client, as we saw in handler.py.

The Query class is the central place where most, if not all, of the functionality, will occur for fetching data from our backend. Our API has two main resources, Session and Cupping. Since we are making this API have functional parity with our REST API, two class attributes will give us the ability to respond to queries for either cuppings or sessions:

```
class Query(graphene.ObjectType):
    sessions = graphene.List(SessionObject,
        id=graphene.Int(), account_id=graphene.Int())
```

```
cuppings = graphene.List(CuppingObject,
    session_id=graphene.Int())

def resolve_cuppings(self, info, **filters):
    return get_cuppings(**filters)

def resolve_sessions(self, info, **filters):
    return get_sessions(**filters)
```

Taking `sessions` as an example, we define the `sessions` attribute to be a list of GraphQL objects, where each item in the list is a `SessionObject`. Fortunately, `SessionObject` is trivial to implement since we can take advantage of Graphene-SQLAlchemy and map the Session SQLAlchemy model to a Graphene-compatible object type. In reality, we could have performed this entirely on our own, but it would have required manually constructing an object that maps SQLAlchemy fields to Graphene fields and writing more code. Graphene-SQLAlchemy handles all of this work automatically.

Two additional keyword arguments are passed into `graphene.List`, id, and `account_id`. Attributes that we want to use to query need to be explicitly defined when building `Query` items. The addition of id and `account_id` mean the API can now accept either or both fields from clients and use them to filter results. Do note that we have surpassed the REST API in functionality, albeit only slightly. By adding `account_id` as a query field, we've given our API new functionality that didn't exist in the REST version. Also, this GraphQL API can return a list of cupping resources, which wasn't possible in the REST API. If you think through the steps of adding this functionality to the REST API, we'd need to add a new endpoint to return the new cupping resources by themselves and either come up with an entirely new API endpoint or shoehorn in some query parameters as GET arguments to filter `Sessions` by account. While either approach can work, it should be clear that this speaks to some of the inconsistencies and areas for interpretation with REST APIs. Here, there is one, and only one, way to add query parameters to a GraphQL query.

Now that we have defined the return values, there is still the work of actually fetching the data. Graphene makes this quite simple by requiring a method prepended with `resolve_` in order to fetch whichever resource we've implemented. The preceding code for both resolve functions, `resolve_sessions`, and `resolve_cuppings`, makes calls to our SQLAlchemy query functions and also passes through any filters that arrive via the extra keyword arguments defined on the `graphene.List` attributes previously described. Both resolve functions will return lists of SQLAlchemy objects; however, because the attributes that are requesting the data are themselves defined as `SQLAlchemyObjectType`, the SQLAlchemy return values are transformed to the correct data types to fulfill the GraphQL queries.

A couple of example queries later in this chapter may help solidify the flow of data and the code.

Implementing GraphQL mutations

After querying comes mutation, which is an operation which writes or otherwise transforms data. In our API, we'll be implementing a single mutation that will create new Session records, which themselves have accompanying cupping records. Again, we're able to reuse helper functions and code to perform some of this work and can focus on the GraphQL code. The following additions to the handlers/graphql.py code implements creating new Session records. There is a slight change to the creation of the schema object, where we pass in a reference to our Mutation class:

```
class CuppingInput(graphene.InputObjectType):
    name = graphene.String(required=True)
    scores = graphene.types.json.JSONString()
    overall_score = graphene.Float(required=True)
    notes = graphene.String()
    descriptors = graphene.List(graphene.String)
    defects = graphene.List(graphene.String)
    is_sample = graphene.Boolean()


class CreateSessionMutation(graphene.Mutation):

    class Arguments:
        name = graphene.String()
        form_name = graphene.String()
        account_id = graphene.Int()
        user_id = graphene.Int()
        cuppings = graphene.List(CuppingInput)

    ok = graphene.Boolean()
    session = graphene.Field(SessionObject)

    def mutate(self, info, *args, **kwargs):
        session = create_session_from_kwargs(kwargs)
        return CreateSessionMutation(session=session, ok=True)


class Mutation(graphene.ObjectType):
    create_session = CreateSessionMutation.Field()
```

```
# Global schema which will handle queries and mutations
schema = graphene.Schema(
        query=Query,
        mutation=Mutation,
        types=[CuppingObject, SessionObject],
)
```

First, notice that the Mutation class is the wrapper around all mutations that need to be defined and passed into our Schema. Just like the Query class, the Mutation class will specify one or more mutation types, which themselves subclass graphene.Mutation. The entry point for a Mutation class is the mutate method.

Before the mutate method can be invoked, the class needs to define a set of input attributes that will accept the actual input data used to create new data. In this case, we need to identify the input data types manually using the raw graphene type. Look at the Arguments class and you should be able to see the one-to-one correspondence with the SQLAlchemy models. GraphQL objects can be nested arbitrarily deep, that can be seen previously, where the cuppings attribute is a list of CuppingInput objects, itself a custom input type specific to our API.

As in the resolve_ functions in a Query attribute, the mutate method delegates the creation of records to an existing SQLAlchemy function ultimately. All of the input data from a client's GraphQL mutation arrive as kwargs to mutate. Those key-value pairs in the form of a Python dictionary are used to create a model, validate, and finally write a new record to the database. At this point, any validation errors are handled by our model layer and error bubble up to the client.

Deployment

With a new Lambda function comes the need to deploy our code, which requires a full deployment via sls deploy. As a reminder, any time you add, remove, or otherwise update an AWS resource, a complete CloudFormation update is needed. We need to add a couple of new entries in the serverless.yml file, which will call the new graphql handler functions:

```
functions:
 GraphQL:
   handler: handler.graphql
   events:
     - http:
         path: graphql
         method: get
```

```
        cors: true
  - http:
      path: graphql
      method: post
      cors: true
```

GraphQL will accept both GET and POST requests, so we'll wire methods to the same /graphql endpoint and make sure we enable CORS.

Since we're using new libraries, Graphene and Graphene-SQLAlchemy, we'll need to update our requirements file and rebuild our supporting libraries. I've added the following library to a specific commit to the requirements.txt file:

git+https://github.com/graphql-python/graphene-sqlalchemy.git@08a0072

Graphene is a requirement for Graphene-SQLAlchemy, so we get both libraries with this single requirement.

We use our Docker container as a build tool:

```
brianz@gold(graphql=)$ ENV=dev make shell
root@7466ff009753:/code#
root@7466ff009753:/code# make libs
pip install -t serverless/lib -r requirements.txt
Collecting git+https://github.com/graphql-python/
  graphene-sqlalchemy.git@08a0072 (from -r requirements.txt
  (line 8))
  Cloning https://github.com/graphql-python/
  graphene-sqlalchemy.git (to 08a0072) to /tmp/pip-3tnr1e2k-build
  Could not find a tag or branch '08a0072', assuming commit.
```

Now, it's safe to do the full deployment, as follows:

```
root@a2484038a502:/code# make deploy
cd serverless && sls deploy -s dev
Serverless: Packaging service...
Serverless: Excluding development dependencies...
Serverless: Uploading CloudFormation file to S3...
Serverless: Uploading artifacts...
Serverless: Uploading service .zip file to S3 (5.55 MB)...
Serverless: Validating template...
Serverless: Updating Stack...
Serverless: Checking Stack update progress...
.........................
Serverless: Stack update finished...
Service Information
service: coffee-cupping
```

```
stage: dev
region: us-west-2
api keys:
None
endpoints:
GET - https://4mvnd1tewe.execute-api.us-west-
     2.amazonaws.com/dev/graphql
POST - https://4mvnd1tewe.execute-api.us-west-
     2.amazonaws.com/dev/graphql
GET - https://4mvnd1tewe.execute-api.us-west-
     2.amazonaws.com/dev/session
POST - https://4mvnd1tewe.execute-api.us-west-
     2.amazonaws.com/dev/session
GET - https://4mvnd1tewe.execute-api.us-west-
     2.amazonaws.com/dev/session/{id}
DELETE - https://4mvnd1tewe.execute-api.us-west-
     2.amazonaws.com/dev/session/{id}
functions:
GraphQL: coffee-cupping-dev-GraphQL
HandleSession: coffee-cupping-dev-HandleSession
HandleSessionDetail: coffee-cupping-dev-HandleSessionDetail
```

With that, we have a new /graphql endpoint, which accepts both GET and POST requests. Next, it's time to test out some GraphQL queries on our serverless endpoint.

 Astute readers may notice the root URL changing between example deployments. During development, this is a frequent occurrence, as you'll often be deploying new stacks and then tearing them down when no longer needed. For each deployment, a unique base URL will be created by API Gateway via CloudFormation. Of course, if this were a production API, you wouldn't be tearing down your serverless stack every evening and rebuilding it in the morning.

Viewing the deployed application

Learning the GraphQL language is a topic in and of itself. In this section, I'll show some queries and mutations using the Insomnia client on macOS. Insomnia is a client application that can be used to make standard REST API requests and also has a lovely GraphQL interface when working with GraphQL endpoints.

A simple query to get a list of cupping sessions, returning only the ID and name of the `Sessions`, looks like the following:

```
query allSessions {
  sessions {
    id
    name
  }
}
```

When you think back to the implementation of the `Query` class, you might recall the following:

```
class Query(graphene.ObjectType):
    sessions = graphene.List(SessionObject, id=graphene.Int(),
        account_id=graphene.Int())
```

Hopefully, things are becoming clearer now. The preceding query is named `allSessions`, and inside it's explicitly asking for `sessions`. Our GraphQL code responds in kind by noticing that the query is for sessions and invoking the `resolve_sessions` function. The following screenshot shows an `allSessions` query using the **Insomnia** client:

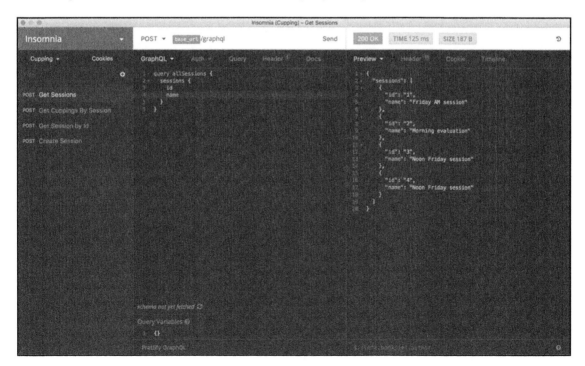

This is great, and the return data may suffice for a client who has a listing of all `Sessions`. But what happens when we want more data? In GraphQL, we merely ask for the data we need. Assume our client application now wants a listing of `Sessions`, but with a few more fields present, including the related `cupping` objects for each `Session`. To accomplish this, we update the query schema that we'll send to the `/graphql` endpoint. Rather than just asking for `id` and `name`, I'll add in `formName`, along with two attributes of the related `cuppings` items:

```
query allSessions {
  sessions {
      id
      name
      formName
        cuppings {
          name
          notes
        }
    }
}
```

The following screenshot shows this query along with the response in the **Insomnia** client:

I have to admit, I was quite excited to see how easy it is to control the output when I got this working. So what if we need to filter some data? Remember the API that didn't exist in our REST API but now does? Let's fetch all of the `cupping` objects that are related to a single `Session`:

```
query Cuppings($sessionId: Int!) {
  cuppings(sessionId: $sessionId) {
    id
    name
    overallScore
    scores
  }
}
```

Again, let's tie this back to our application code and remember what the `cuppings` attribute was in our `Query`, class. Inside `Query` we have the following:

```
cuppings = graphene.List(CuppingObject,
    session_id=graphene.Int())
```

Graphene does include some magic for auto *CamelCase* input and output data. Even though the `cuppings` attribute specifies `session_id` as an input filter, the client uses `SessionId`. The end result is that the Python code receives `session_id` as a keyword argument that is passed to the SQLAlchemy query. The end result is that SQLAlchemy performs a query analogous to the following SQL statement:

```
select * from cuppings where session_id = 1
```

The following screenshot shows a GraphQL query that will fetch a single `Session` based on a numeric ID from our GraphQL API:

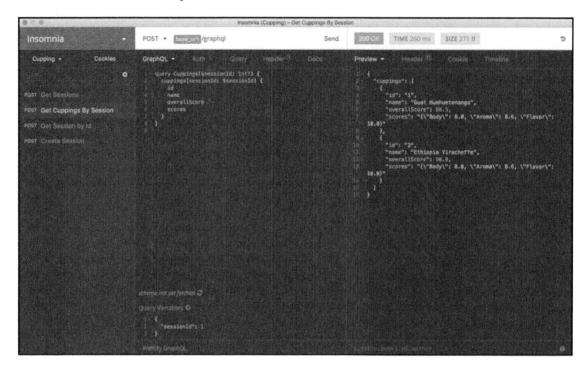

Finally, let's take a look at the mutation portion of our code and create some new data. You might expect this to be fairly simple, and it is for the most part. One slight complication is that the cupping scores field in the database is a PostgreSQL JSONB type, which allows for maximum flexibility. Inputting JSON requires escaping this field, which is the reason for all of the backslashes in the mutation request. The following code snippet is a GraphQL mutation that creates a new `Session` record:

```
mutation CreateSession {
  createSession (
    name: "Noon Friday session"
    formName: "Roastery custom"
    accountId: 234
    cuppings: [
    {
      name: "Ethiopia Cochere"
      overallScore: 91
      scores: "{\"Aroma\": 10, \"Flavor\": 9, \"Body\": 8,
            \"Clean Cup\": 6}"
```

```
          descriptors: ["port-wine" "chocolate"]
          notes: "deep and dark"
        }
      ]
    )
    {
      ok
      session {
        id
        name
        formName
        cuppings {
          sessionId
          name
          overallScore
          scores
          defects
          descriptors
          notes
        }
      }
    }
  }
```

I won't go through all of the application code, but at a high level, our request sends in a
`createSession` mutation to the application. This input payload maps directly to our
`create_session` attribute on the `Mutation` class thanks to the auto *CamelCasing* from
Graphene:

```
class Mutation(graphene.ObjectType):
    create_session = CreateSessionMutation.Field()
```

The input data in the preceding mutation is reasonably small. What is more verbose is the
section for the return values. Our mutation returns an `ok` attribute, which is a Boolean,
along with the newly created `Session` resource. Because of that, our mutation can request
precisely what it needs from the newly created resource.

The following screenshot shows the input and output when creating a new `Session` record in the Insomnia client:

GraphQL has much more to offer, and I only wish there was more time to cover it.

Iteration and deployment

While developing this code using the existing repository, I repeatedly needed to update just the GraphQL portion of the stack. Using the Serverless Framework and its ability to update a single Lambda function made this very easy. With the shortcut in the `Makefile`, deploying a single function looks like the following:

```
root@7466ff009753:/code# make deploy function=GraphQL
cd serverless && sls deploy function -s dev -f GraphQL
Serverless: Packaging function: GraphQL...
Serverless: Excluding development dependencies...
Serverless: Uploading function: GraphQL (5.74 MB)...
Serverless: Successfully deployed function: GraphQL
root@7466ff009753:/code# make deploy
```

It's hard to give exact numbers, but deployments like this after iteration on code take in the order of two-five seconds. Deployment speed will mostly depend on your upload speeds and the final size of the application package.

Of course, iterating and adding new code means writing more tests. Serverless applications can be slightly tricky since it's possible to write a rich set of unit tests, only to see the deployed application fail due to missing or presumptuous tests higher up in the stack. My advice is to write the right mix of unit tests, without being academic about it, along with a very rich set of integration tests as the highest level of code that is practical.

Using a concrete example, this GraphQL query and mutation code above is 100% tested, as is the `cupping.handlers.graphql.handle_graphql` function. This strategy ensures that all of the error handling, JSON decoding of the payload, and other utility code is behaving as expected, in addition to testing the GraphQL business logic.

Summary

In this chapter, we walked through the entire process of creating a three-tier web application with a serverless architecture using a GraphQL interface. The vast majority of this application is similar to the REST version of the same application. We learned the changes needed to migrate from a REST interface and design to a GraphQL design, both from the perspective of application code and serverless functions.

Readers should now have a high-level understanding of the advantages of employing a GraphQL interface in a serverless architecture and have enough knowledge to begin implementation of their own serverless GraphQL application.

In `Chapter 4`, *Integrating Legacy APIs with the Proxy Pattern*, we will work through yet another web application pattern for proxying API requests from clients through a serverless application to a legacy API.

4

Integrating Legacy APIs with the Proxy Pattern

Developing a new API is very often a pleasant experience for developers. Without any legacy code, we engineers can choose our tooling, think through the design process to ensure an enjoyable end user experience, build on top of a serverless platform, and all of the other best practices learned through the ages. However, companies and bosses task many engineers with taking a legacy API and supporting, maintaining, or porting it to a new architecture. Given an already deployed production API that sees constant usage, porting to a serverless system can be akin to changing the engine of a race car while in the middle of a race.

Fortunately, this complicated task can be made much simpler nowadays using the proxy pattern, the idea of which has been around for many years as a software pattern. If the name isn't clear enough, the main ideas are that a layer sits in between the client and backend system, which acts as a proxy, shuffling data to and from the backend service on behalf of the client. Inserting this proxy in between the two actors (client and server) makes it possible to transform request data from the client before it's sent to the server, as well as transform the payload from the server before it's delivered to the client. In this manner, one may mimic the exact behavior of a legacy API without any changes needed on the client side. This design allows for a graceful transition from a legacy API backend to a newer backend system without the fear of breaking existing clients or requiring them to update their application.

By the end of this chapter, you can expect to learn the following:

- Introduction to the proxy pattern and how it works for migrating API backends or updating the request/response payloads for existing APIs
- Options for implementing the proxy pattern, including AWS API Gateway and custom serverless functions

- Transforming requests/responses to an existing API
- Migrating existing APIs to a serverless backend

AWS API Gateway introduction

API Gateway from Amazon Web Services is a fantastic tool with a slew of features that significantly simplifies implementation of an API proxy pattern. Later on in the chapter, we'll discuss strategies when building on a different cloud provider; however, if you're like me and use AWS consistently, API Gateway can make your life much more comfortable. Personally, I feel that it's an underrated tool, which can do a lot more than HTTP requests to Lambda functions as we saw in Chapter 2, *Three-Tier Web Application Using REST* and Chapter 3, *Three-Tier Web Application Pattern with GraphQL*.

The first question may be, *What is API Gateway and what does it do?* Rather than answer this myself, I'll defer to the technical documentation at http://docs.aws.amazon.com/apigateway/latest/developerguide/welcome.html, which does a good job of describing Gateway at a high level:

> *"Amazon API Gateway is an AWS service that enables developers to create, publish, maintain, monitor, and secure APIs at any scale. You can create APIs that access AWS or other web services, as well as data stored in the AWS Cloud."*

API Gateway provides you with a publicly accessible HTTPS URL. Requests that hit this endpoint may do a variety of things including, but not limited to, the following:

- Call a Lambda function
- Return a mock endpoint build with templates
- Proxy requests to a different HTTP endpoint

In Chapter 2, *A Three-Tier Web Application Using REST* and Chapter 3, *A Three-Tier Web Application Pattern with GraphQL*, we used API Gateway to expose an HTTPS endpoint that would invoke our Lambda functions containing application logic. HTTP payload data, including headers and query parameters, would be pulled in from the HTTPS request and sent to Lambda. Our Lambda functions also control the response payload by returning a JSON-encodable data structure as well as appropriate HTTP status codes and headers. Managing the actual HTTP response from Lambda is known as a **proxy integration**, not to be confused with the proxy pattern we will work on in this chapter. I bring this up to add clarity to what we've done and what we'll be doing for this pattern with API Gateway.

In most of the subsequent examples, we will not be using the Lambda proxy integration. While this means more configuration will work on our behalf, it also means we will be able to control the request/response payloads to our liking. When building a brand new Serverless API with API Gateway and AWS Lambda, Lambda proxy integration should be precisely what you need since it's easy to control requests and responses from your API definition and application code, respectively. However, when setting up the proxy pattern for an existing HTTP backend, it's common to need more control over transforming response data before it's sent back to the client.

In addition to being the ingestion point for web requests and sending those requests somewhere else, API Gateway provides quite a bit more functionality, including:

- Authentication and authorization hooks
- Automatic API documentation generation
- Rate limiting/throttling
- Logging
- Defining multiple stages or environments with their variables that can be passed to downstream systems

Personally speaking, the more I learn about the capabilities of API Gateway, the more ideas I come up with for possible applications and use cases.

 There are other services that provide similar functionality. If you prefer to build on something other than AWS, have a look at **Apigee** (`https://apigee.com/api-management/`) or **Kong** (`https://getkong.org/`).

Simple proxy to a legacy API

In this first example, we'll go through the steps to set up a simple integration with an existing API. What is neat about API Gateway is that it's possible to go a very long way on the path to replacing current application code without writing any code ourselves.

In these examples, we'll use a publicly available fake API called `JsonPlaceholder`, pretending for our purposes that it's a legacy API that we'd like to replace: `https://jsonplaceholder.typicode.com`.

Of course, this type of replacement warrants plenty of thought and careful planning. Authentication, rate limiting, DNS entries, and the like are all factors that much be thought through carefully before embarking on such a project. Still, with all of the issues that one should consider, there are many tools and options to make this pattern a real possibility for many applications.

Setting up a pass-through proxy

Step one on our journey will be to work through the steps of setting up a new API in API Gateway that will pass requests and responses to and from `JsonPlaceholder`.

First, in the AWS console, create a new API, shown as follows. I'll call this one `JsonProxy`:

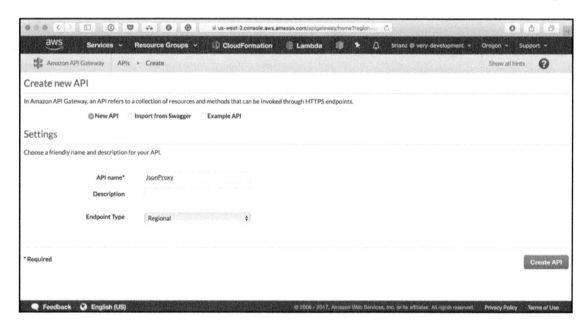

Once we have our API, we can start filling it in and adding endpoints and behavior. In my experience, most AWS services have essential concepts that one should understand well before building something of significance. API Gateway is no different in this regard. The good news is that it's not incredibly difficult to understand these concepts in API Gateway.

The two concepts we'll be working with when using API Gateway are resources and methods. The mental model is situation simple:

- **Resource**: API endpoint
- **Method**: HTTP method that lives under a resource

`JSONPlaceholder` provides API endpoints for a few different API resources, posts, comments, albums, and so on. To begin, we'll create a new API Gateway resource for `/posts`. This endpoint, on our unique URL, will proxy to `https://jsonplaceholder.typicode.com/posts`. It should be noted that we could set up an endpoint on our API Gateway deployment named something other than `/posts`. That is, it's possible to create a resource named `/all_posts`, which would then proxy to `https://jsonplaceholder.typicode.com/posts`.

In the console, we set this up in the following way:

1. Select the **Actions** button → **Create Resource**:
   1. Set **Resource Name** to be **posts**
   2. Ensure **Configure as proxy resource** is not checked
   3. Click the **Create Resource** button
2. Ensure the newly created `/posts` resource is selected/highlighted in the list of resources

3. Select the **Actions** button → **Create Method**:
    1. Select **GET** and click the confirmation checkbox button
    2. On the next screen, set the options as shown in the following screenshot
    3. Ensure the **Endpoint URL** is pointing to `https://jsonplaceholder.typicode.com/posts`
    4. Click the **Save** button; take a look at the following screenshot:

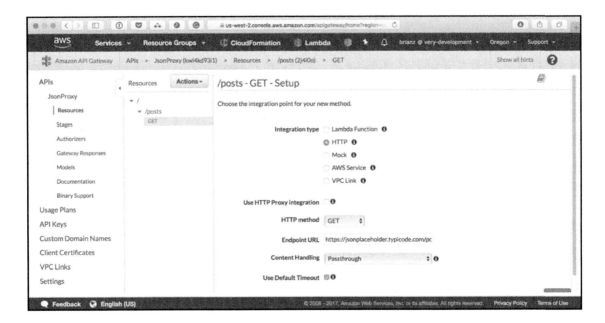

The preceding screenshot may look quite confusing. I'll admit, I didn't understand many details of this part of API Gateway for quite a long time until I went through this exercise that we're going through now. We'll go through the details of the **Method Execution** screen in detail, but first, let's deploy our new API and test it out:

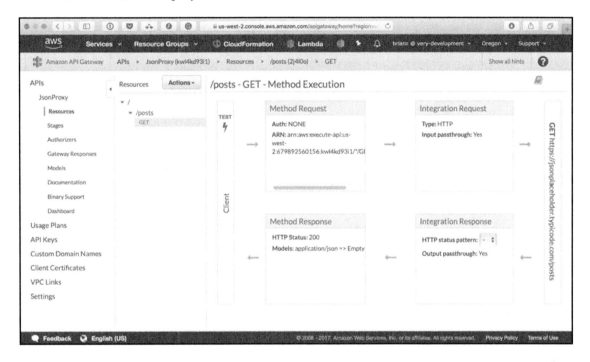

Deploying a pass-through proxy

At this point, we've merely defined our API's skeleton and straightforward structure, with a single endpoint of /posts. There is no URL for us to query to test. For that, we'll need to deploy our API:

1. Select the Actions button → **Deploy API**
2. From the **Deploy API** screen:
    1. Select **New stage**
    2. Enter dev for the stage name
3. Click the **Deploy** button

After deployment, the console will take you to the **dev Stage Editor** screen. Here, you'll notice many other types of features that you can update. For example, it's possible to turn on/off API throttling, set stage variables, and so on. For our purposes, we're all done:

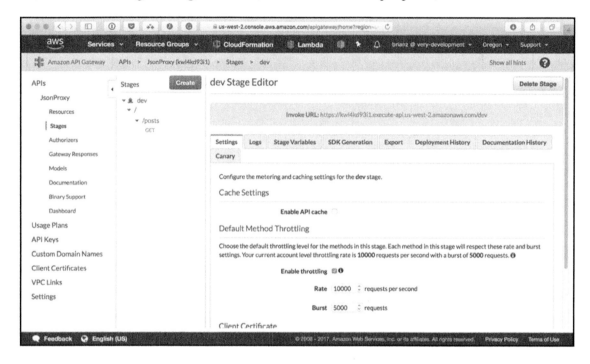

You'll notice a URL highlighted at the top of this screen. This custom URL is unique to this deployment and may be used to hit our API. Expanding the **dev** stage on the left-hand side will show you the single URL endpoint we defined in the prior **Resources** section.

Now, if we load up our custom URL in the browser or hit that URL with cURL, we can see the data pulled from the JSONPlaceholder endpoint of /posts:

```
$ curl https://kwl4kd93i1.execute-api.us-west-2.amazonaws.com/dev/posts
[
  {
    "userId": 1,
    "id": 1,
    "title": "sunt aut facere repellat provident occaecati excepturi optio reprehenderit",
    "body": "quia et suscipit\nsuscipit recusandae consequuntur expedita et cum\nreprehenderit molestiae ut ut quas totam\nnostrum rerum est autem sunt rem eveniet architecto"
  },
```

```
{
    "userId": 1,
    "id": 2,
    "title": "qui est esse",
    "body": "est rerum tempore vitae\nsequi sint nihil reprehenderit dolor
beatae ea dolores neque\nfugiat blanditiis voluptate porro vel nihil
molestiae ut reiciendis\nqui aperiam non debitis possimus qui neque nisi
nulla"
    }...
]
```

What we have now is our very own HTTPS URL, which doesn't do much, but it's still quite remarkable. We have not written a single line of application code in any sort of programming language, and have set up a proxy to return results from an existing legacy API. You may think this isn't very useful right now. You wouldn't be wrong, necessarily. However, even with a simple integration like this, we can already begin to take advantage of some API Gateway features such as:

- Automated API documentation generation
- Throttling
- Automated SDK generation in multiple languages

This is merely the first step. In the next section, we will dive into the details of starting to transform our API Gateway API to turn it into something completely different using the same data source.

Transforming responses from a modern API

Next, we'll walk through a scenario where we have an existing API interface that we need to support, but would like to change the backend implementation entirely. This scenario is common and one I've dealt with personally. Existing clients point to a particular set of API endpoints. Breaking a public API that many developers depend on isn't something anyone wants to do. But, when that API is built on top of hard-to-maintain or poorly performing code, how does one iterate without requiring hundreds or thousands of developers to update their mobile, web, or GUI applications?

In this example, I will walk through the steps necessary to take a pretend legacy API and reimplement it using our modern API. JSONPlaceholder will play the part of our new, modern, scalable, and performant RESTful API. The single URL we will reimplement with the proxy pattern is https://$HOSTNAME/get_comments_by_post_id.

You can imagine the type of data this endpoint returns. Thinking back to our discussion on REST APIs, it's evident that this legacy pattern is not RESTful for a variety of reasons. With an API structure such as this, you can bet that the rest of the API design will need some work and may not be the easiest to work with as an end user. Our shiny new RESTful API (`JSONPlaceholder`) is much more to our liking and one that we'd like to advertise and have developers adopt rather than the previous old structure. How can we support existing clients with the same input and output payloads by using our new RESTful API?

API Gateway can help us out in this scenario.

Method execution flow

The **Method Execution** screenshot shown in the *Setting up a pass-through proxy* section will come into play now. You may refer back to that screenshot as we walk through the four different parts. It also may be easier to look at the following diagram, which represents the same request/response flow but is a bit simpler to digest:

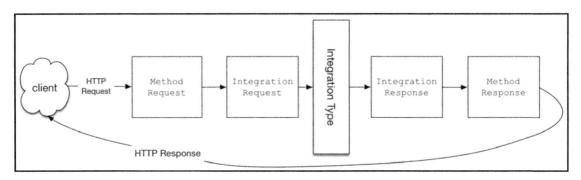

For every API Gateway resource/method combination, there are four steps that we may configure. It all starts with the client on the far left of this diagram. This **client** icon represents the user who is calling our API. After a series of steps, an HTTP response is created, and the client receives some payload. Working with API Gateway means configuring some or all of these stages to control the HTTP request and the HTTP response. Sitting right in the middle of this flow is the **Integration Type**, which, as mentioned earlier, may be a variety of things, including an AWS Lambda function or existing HTTP endpoint. The two steps that precede the execution of the integration (**Method Request** and **Integration Request**) are responsible for working with the HTTP request. The work that these two stages perform may include:

- Transforming query parameters
- Transforming input data (that is, POST payload)

- Extracting and transforming headers
- Performing authentication

Once this work is done, the **Integration Request** will pass data (which may or may not be transformed from the original input payload) to the **Integration Type**. The **Integration Type** returns some data, hands it off to the **Integration Response**, and finally **Method Response**. As the other two sections worked on the request payload, these two sections (**Integration Response** and **Method Response**) operate on the response payload. Actions we may perform here include:

- Transforming the HTTP body/payload
- Transforming/adding HTTP headers
- Controlling HTTP status codes

In the AWS console screenshot in the *Setting up a pass-through proxy* section, the client is represented on the far left as a vertically oriented rectangle. On the far right of the same screenshot is the endpoint that we configured this API to talk with, `https://jsonplaceholder.typicode.com/posts`. Again, in other cases, that integration endpoint may be a Lambda function, mock integration, or any of the other supported backend systems for API Gateway. In our example for this chapter, it will always be our existing `JSONPlaceholder` API. Following the arrows in the **Method Execution** screen on the AWS console you can see how a request from clients flows in the order described previously:

- Method Request
- Integration Request
- Our configured integration endpoint
- Integration Response
- Method Response

There are many options and a huge number of permutations with this flow of data. We can't go through every one obviously, but we'll work primarily with Integration Request and Integration Response for this example. Our tasks will involve:

- Creating new resources for the three separate legacy API endpoints
- Creating `GET` methods on those three resources
- For each resource/method combination, map query parameters from the request to our new API
- For each resource/method combination, set up an Integration Response Body Mapping Template to transform the JSON payload from our new API to the structure expected of the legacy API

Setting up example

The API to integrate with has the URL structure of `https://jsonplaceholder.typicode.com/comments?postId=1`. As a reminder, this is the endpoint URL for our HTTP Integration Type. With a URL structure like that, it's clear what is going on and what the return data should be. This request fetches comments for a given `postId`, which are passed along as a `GET` argument. Additionally, this modern API returns an array of comment resources with the following format:

```
{
  "postId": 1,
  "id": 1,
  "name": "id labore ex et quam laborum",
  "email": "Eliseo@gardner.biz",
  "body": "laudantium enim quasi est quidem magnam voluptate ipsam
eos\ntempora quo necessitatibus\ndolor quam autem quasi\nreiciendis et
nam sapiente accusantium"
}
```

Assume for the sake of this example that our legacy system has an analogous API but with a different URL structure, `GET` argument to filter the comments and representation of the comment resource:

```
https://$HOSTNAME/get_comments_by_post_id?post_id=1
```

```
{
  "comment_id": 1,
  "name": "id labore ex et quam laborum",
  "user": {
    email": "Eliseo@gardner.biz"
  },
  "text": "laudantium enim quasi est quidem magnam voluptate ipsam
eos\ntempora quo necessitatibus\ndolor quam autem quasi\nreiciendis et
nam sapiente accusantium"
}
```

Our job here is to support this legacy URL pattern and payload using the modern-day RESTful API (`JSONPlaceholder`) as the data source. Fortunately, all of the data we need to support we have in our new API, so our job will be to have API Gateway perform the translation of the payload before it's sent out to the client.

Setting up a new resource and method

First, we need to create a new API Gateway resource and method for the `get_comments_by_post_id` endpoint. The steps are the same as the prior section. The only differences will be:

- The endpoint we'll talk to will be `https://jsonplaceholder.typicode.com/comments` rather than the `/posts` endpoint
- We'll need to map query parameters from the initial client request to the desired query parameters to the backend API that provides the data

After setting up this new resource and method, it should look like the following:

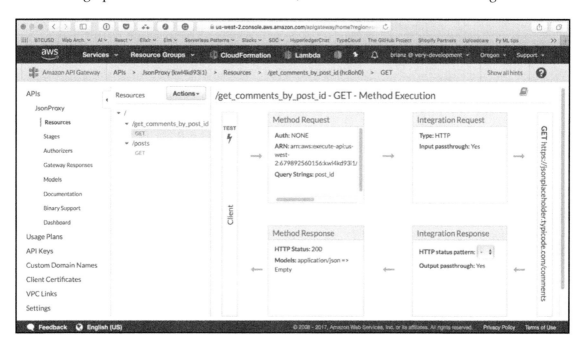

Setting up Integration Request

First, we need to set up API Gateway so that it passes the expected GET arguments from the request to our backend. API Gateway allows for controlling the query parameter mapping in the *Method Request* and *Integration Request* sections. In the **Method Execution** screen:

1. Click on Method Request:
    1. Click on **URL Query String Parameters**
    2. Click **Add query string parameter**
    3. Put in post_id
    4. Leave **required** and **caching** unchecked
2. Back on the **Method Execution** screen, click on **Integration Request**:
    1. Expand **URL Query String Parameters**
    2. Click on **Add query string**
    3. Put in postId for
       Name and method.request.querystring.post_id for **Mapped from**

What we've done here is tell API Gateway to expect a GET argument named post_id, which is the old parameter we need to support. From there, Gateway will extract this post_id attribute and inject it into the Integration Request. The value for post_id is accessible in method.request.querystring.post_id.

By adding a new query string named postId and with a value of method.request.querystring.post_id, we're simply passing that value along to the new RESTful API, but using the new parameter name of postId:

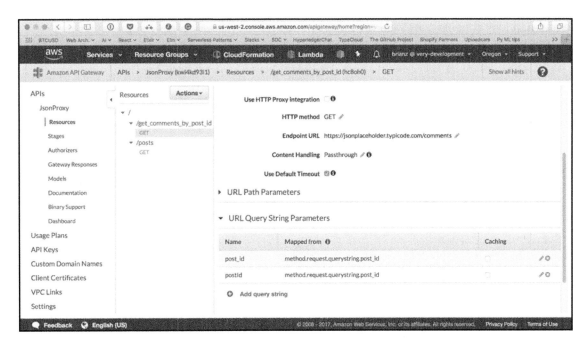

To test these changes, we need to deploy the API. In the console, in the **Resources** section, select the **Actions** button and click **Deploy API**. Deploy this to our single `dev` stage:

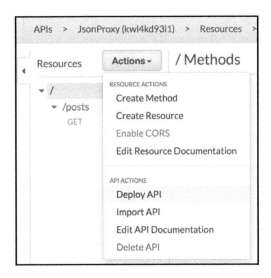

We can hit our new API and see the results using `curl`:

```
$ curl
https://kwl4kd93i1.execute-api.us-west-2.amazonaws.com/dev/get_comments_by_
post_id?post_id=10
[
  {
    "postId": 10,
    "id": 46,
    "name": "dignissimos et deleniti voluptate et quod",
    "email": "Jeremy.Harann@waino.me",
    "body": "exercitationem et id quae cum omnis\nvoluptatibus accusantium
et quidem\nut ipsam sint\ndoloremque illo ex atque necessitatibus sed"
  },
  {
    "postId": 10,
    "id": 47,
    "name": "rerum commodi est non dolor nesciunt ut",
    "email": "Pearlie.Kling@sandy.com",
    "body": "occaecati laudantium ratione non cumque\nearum quod non enim
soluta nisi velit similique voluptatibus\nesse laudantium consequatur
voluptatem rem eaque voluptatem aut ut\net sit quam"
  },
  ...
]
```

Setting up Integration Response

Now that we have the URL and query parameter mapping working, it's time to begin transforming the response generated from our new API. Since the old JSON structure is different, we'll use Gateway's Body Mapping Templates to take the output from the JSON response and rewrite it. API Gateway uses the Velocity Template language and system to perform this work. If you've ever done web programming with a modern-day web framework, you've undoubtedly worked with a templating library. There are many. Velocity isn't magic; it serves the same purpose as any other templating system: taking some marked up template in a particular syntax along with some contextual data and rendering an output string.

In the **Method Execution** screen, click on **Integration Response**. Where we are at this point in the request/response cycle is after the backend integration has generated a response, just before the system starts sending the data back to the client. At this stage, we'll configure the Integration Response to rewrite the output to the client using two things:

- The JSON response from our backend (JSONPlaceholder)
- A body mapping template, which is written using the Velocity Template language

In this section, it's possible to set up different body mapping templates based on HTTP response codes and content/type. For simplicity, we'll just be dealing with HTTP 200 and a single **Integration Response**, response code, and content/type.

In the **Integration Response** section:

1. Expand the single row in the table, which is the **Default mapping**
2. Expand the **Body Mapping Templates** section
3. Click on the **application/json** in the **Content-Type** table
4. Add the following template code in the text area and click **Save**
5. Deploy the API to the dev stage

The code block as follows refers to step #4. This is the Velocity Template language syntax:

```
#set($inputRoot = $input.path('$'))
#foreach ($comment in $inputRoot)
{
  "comment_id": $comment.id,
  "name": "$comment.name",
  "user": {
    "email": "$comment.email"
  },
  "text": "$comment.body"
}
#end
```

The template code in the preceding code block should be placed in the template section for the **application/json**, **Content-Type**, as shown in the screenshot as follows:

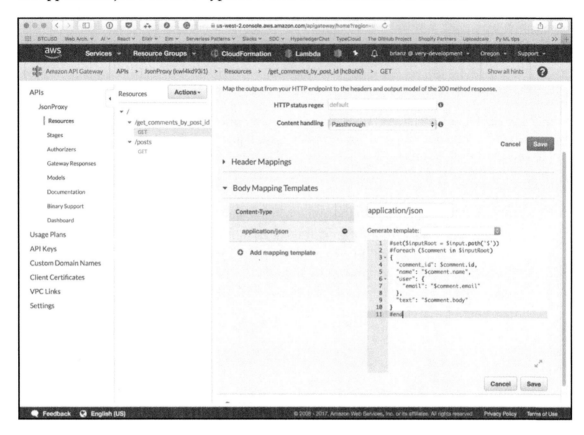

With that out of the way, calling our API will result in a completely different structure of the return payload:

```
$ curl
https://kwl4kd93i1.execute-api.us-west-2.amazonaws.com/dev/get_comments_by_
post_id?post_id=10
{
  "comment_id": 1,
  "name": "id labore ex et quam laborum",
  "user": {
    "email": "Eliseo@gardner.biz"
  },
  "text": "laudantium enim quasi est quidem magnam voluptate ipsam eos
tempora quo necessitatibus
dolor quam autem quasi
```

```
reiciendis et nam sapiente accusantium"
}
{
  "comment_id": 2,
  "name": "quo vero reiciendis velit similique earum",
  "user": {
    "email": "Jayne_Kuhic@sydney.com"
  },
  "text": "est natus enim nihil est dolore omnis voluptatem numquam
et omnis occaecati quod ullam at
voluptatem error expedita pariatur
nihil sint nostrum voluptatem reiciendis et"
}
```

Provided the backend system contains the necessary data, it's possible to implement a complete API with an entirely different structure, writing nothing more than some API Gateway configuration and Velocity Templates. As mentioned earlier, there are many other advantages to API Gateway that you can leverage, which may be extremely useful when replacing a legacy API.

Complex integration using a Lambda function

Our prior example is a best-case scenario. Because our new backend system included all of the data we needed to support our legacy API, our jobs were pretty easy. However, what happens in cases where the legacy API you need to support does not have a one-to-one mapping with a newer API? Of course, if you control the new API it's possible to implement any missing functionality. While that may be possible, it may not be a good idea since you may be reimplementing imperfect design in your new and clean RESTful API in order to support a legacy system.

In this case, rather than dirtying the new API, it's possible to use a Lambda function as the Integration Type, rather than an HTTP endpoint. With this pattern, the Lambda function may act with some intelligence and perform any type of task that is needed. For example, imagine another legacy endpoint of `https://$HOSTNAME/get_posts_with_users` that returns a list of `posts` with the `user` records embedded in each post record. The new API returns `posts` with a structure as follows:

```
{
  "userId": 1,
  "id": 5,
  "title": "nesciunt quas odio",
```

```
    "body": "repudiandae veniam quaerat..."
},
```

However, our legacy API needs that payload to be returned in the form of the following:

```
{
    "title" : "nesciunt quas odio",
    "id" : 5,
    "user" : {
        "id" : 1,
        "name" : "Leanne Graham",
        "phone" : "1-770-736-8031 x56442",
        "email" : "Sincere@april.biz",
        "username" : "Bret",
        "address" : {
            "suite" : "Apt. 556",
            "street" : "Kulas Light",
            "city" : "Gwenborough",
            "zipcode" : "92998-3874"
        }
    },
    "body" : "repudiandae veniam quaerat..."
}
```

The new API has the user data available at the /users endpoint. Using a Lambda function, we can make two separate API calls and mash up the results ourselves.

Implementing the application code

First, we need to implement our application logic. The code will be very straightforward and I won't cover the details. Everything can be implemented in a mere 42 lines of Python code:

```python
import json

import sys
from pathlib import Path

# Munge our sys path so libs can be found
CWD = Path(__file__).resolve().cwd() / 'lib'
sys.path.insert(0, str(CWD))

import requests


def get_users(event, context):
```

```
        user_response =
requests.get('https://jsonplaceholder.typicode.com/users')
        users = {}
        for user in user_response.json():
            users[user['id']] = user

        post_response =
requests.get('https://jsonplaceholder.typicode.com/posts')
        posts = []
        for post in post_response.json():
            user = users[post['userId']]
            posts.append({
                "id" : post['id'],
                "body" : post['body'],
                "title" : post['title'],
                "user" : {
                    "id" : user['id'],
                    "name" : user['name'],
                    "phone" : user['phone'],
                    "email" : user['email'],
                    "username" : user['username'],
                    "address" : user['address'],
                }
            })

    response = {
        "statusCode": 200,
        "body": json.dumps(posts)
    }

    return response
```

Now that our application logic is making the two HTTP requests to our backend and mashing up the results, we finally have our desired output format, where `user` records are embedded in the `post` records.

Deploying this consists of setting up a serverless *service* with a single endpoint. Interestingly, we'll define our function in `serverless.yml` but will not use any event to trigger this function. The reason for this is that we will manually set up this function to be triggered by our existing API Gateway deployment:

```
service: api-proxy

provider:
  name: aws
  runtime: python3.6
  region: ${env:AWS_DEFAULT_REGION}
```

```
functions:
  GetUsers:
    handler: handler.get_users
```

Setting up a new resource and method

Now, it's time to set up a new resource and GET method in API Gateway. This time, we'll select **Lambda Function** as the **Integration type**. Also, we will want to check **Use Lambda Proxy integration**. The reason for choosing this now is that we can control details of the response from our application code run by Lambda. If there is a need to update headers or otherwise transform the response, we simply update our application code and redeploy the Lambda function:

Select the already deployed Lambda function, click **Save**, and we're all done. There is no need to update the **Method Request** or **Integration** since we may perform any transformations from the application code.

Finally, deploy the API, hit the new API endpoint, and see the results:

```
[
    {
        "title" : "sunt aut facere repellat provident occaecati excepturi
optio reprehenderit",
        "id" : 1,
        "body" : "quia et suscipit\nsuscipit recusandae consequuntur
expedita et cum\nreprehenderit molestiae ut ut quas totam\nnostrum
rerum est autem sunt rem eveniet architecto",
        "user" : {
            "name" : "Leanne Graham",
            "email" : "Sincere@april.biz",
            "username" : "Bret",
            "id" : 1,
            "address" : {
                "geo" : {
                    "lng" : "81.1496",
                    "lat" : "-37.3159"
                },
                "suite" : "Apt. 556",
                "city" : "Gwenborough",
                "street" : "Kulas Light",
                "zipcode" : "92998-3874"
            },
            "phone" : "1-770-736-8031 x56442"
        }
    },
    ...
}
```

Migration techniques

In these examples, we've taken a look at a few strategies for implementing a new API using existing API backends. Another common scenario is migrating an *existing* API to a serverless architecture, *without* changing any of its functionality. In this scenario, we can still use the proxy pattern and API Gateway. With all of the work in place ready to go, how does one actually deploy a new proxy layer without affecting existing traffic or breaking these clients? The following are a few techniques and deployment strategies that you may consider when faced with this problem.

Staged migration

To replace an existing API with a serverless-based system, it makes sense to first implement the proxy pattern and define the complete API in API Gateway. Each endpoint would simply proxy requests and responses to and from their corresponding APIs on the system to be replaced.

It's even possible to start initial testing with what is called a **proxy resource**. With this model, one creates a resource in API Gateway named {proxy+}. This is a greedy resource and will match any URL path that doesn't already exist, be it /cats, /users/10/comments, and so on. It will also match on any HTTP verb. In short, it's a catch-all that will send any request that doesn't match an existing resource on to the configure Integration backend:

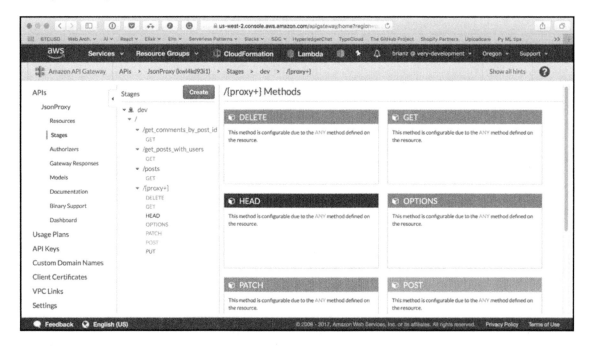

Doing this first is a good way to start testing the interaction between Gateway and your backend system since you can build out a full test suite without the fear of misconfiguring anything. Slowly, you may begin implementing and replacing different APIs one by one. In this fashion, you can work at your own pace without the fear of flipping a switch to move *all* APIs to some new system at once. If a single deployment of a new serverless API doesn't go well, rolling back takes mere seconds by deleting the resource and redeploying the API. Since the proxy resource will catch any non-matching URL paths, deleting a problematic resource simply points that URL path back to the original HTTP integration endpoint. This is as simple of a rollback procedure as you'll find.

Migrating URLs

You may have noticed that the URLs provided by API Gateway are quite obscure and not easy to remember, for example, `https://eocmzivub6.execute-api.us-west-2.amazonaws.com`. In the example of replacing a legacy API from under existing users, the ideal scenario is to merely update DNS records.

For example, presume the API you're migrating is located at `https://api.mysite.io` and that this URL is embedded across thousands of devices in a mobile application. Forcing users to update their code isn't feasible with thousands of clients. You know that there will be traffic to that subdomain for a long time.

API Gateway provides the ability to apply a custom domain to an API and provides free SSL/TLS certificates. With those two features, a migration would be fairly straightforward. Assuming you've implemented and thoroughly tested the new API Gateway version of your API, the migration would consist of:

- Setting up `api.mysite.io` as a custom domain in API Gateway
- Creating a TLS certificate for `api.mysite.io` from API Gateway (using Amazon Certificate Manager, ACM)
- Updating DNS to point to the API Gateway URL

In cases where the URL is not running on a subdomain, life becomes more complex. For example, if you have an existing web application running at `https://mysite.io` and the API is found at `https://mysite.io/api`, changing DNS would not work since it would break it for the users of your web application. In this case, there are two viable options:

- Use or set up some type of router or load balancer that supports path-based routing

- Update application code to call the API Gateway endpoints for any request to
  `/api`

A load balancer such as HAProxy would work out well here since it provides path-based routing and is extremely fast. If it's not feasible to set up a system such as that, a final solution would be to manually proxy requests from your own application code to the API Gateway endpoint. That method isn't elegant, but technically it would work provided headers and query parameters are forwarded along to API Gateway.

Summary

In this chapter, we introduced the proxy pattern using API Gateway from AWS. We walked through multiple examples of mimicking a legacy API using an existing RESTful URL as an HTTP integration. You learned the four stages of API Gateway method execution and some of the details surrounding each of those integration points. We also discussed the proxy pattern when integrating with an AWS Lambda function, which provides a bit more control at the expense of more maintenance.

Readers should understand the proxy pattern and have a rough idea of how to implement this themselves using API Gateway after this chapter.

In the next chapter, we'll move our focus from web application patterns to those for data processing.

5
Scaling Out with the Fan-Out Pattern

The next turn in our serverless journey takes us away from web-centric patterns and towards those suitable for a variety of problems, web and otherwise. In this chapter, we'll discuss the fan-out pattern, which may be used in many different contexts, either by itself as a standalone system or within a larger project as a sub-unit. Conceptually, the fan-out pattern is precisely what it sounds like—one serverless entry point results in multiple invocations of downstream systems. Big data platforms and computer science algorithms have been using this trick for a very long time; by taking a sizable computational problem and breaking it into smaller pieces, a system can get to the result faster by working on those smaller pieces concurrently. Conceptually, this is precisely how MapReduce works in the mapping step.

In this chapter, we will discuss how to split a single unit of work into multiple smaller groups of work using the fan-out pattern. We will go through use cases for this pattern and the various problems for which it's well suited.

By the end of this chapter, you can expect to know the following:

- How to set up a fan-out architecture for resizing images in parallel
- How to use the fan-out pattern to split a single large input file into smaller files and process those pieces in parallel
- What types of problem is the fan-out pattern is suitable for?

System architecture

In many ways, this is the most straightforward pattern covered in this book. A single entry point, whether it be an HTTP request, some event notification, or anything else supported on your cloud provider of choice, triggers multiple invocations of some other serverless function in parallel. What one gains in this architecture is parallelism and hence speed. Our first example is one which is easy to understand and which you can view as the `Hello World` of serverless architectures.

Imagine a system which takes an image and creates multiple versions of the original image with different sizes smaller than the original. How can this be solved at its simplest? Once a user uploads an image, our system notices the new image upload and, using a `for` loop, iterates and creates the various thumbnails. Some fictitious code to do this may look like the following:

```
const sizes = [128, 256, 512, 1024];
const img = readSomeImage();

sizes.forEach(function(size) {
   img.resize(size, AUTO);
})
```

This can work just fine but runs the risk of slowing down drastically as a single process is in charge of the entire pipeline for one image. Logically speaking, each resize event is completely independent, only depending on the original image to perform its task. As such, this is a perfect task to run in parallel. The following diagram shows the general design for the fan-out pattern, where a single entry point triggers multiple downstream processes:

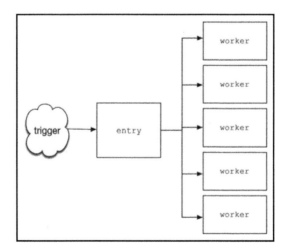

Some event or trigger will result in a call to an entry point function. In the image resize example, this event occurs when an image is uploaded to an AWS S3 bucket. Admittedly, setting this up is very simple, and AWS makes the invocation of Lambda functions quite easy due to all their cross-service integrations. However, one may apply this pattern to any cloud provider, and the trigger could very well be the uploading of an image over an HTTP POST rather than to an S3 bucket. Once the entry function is invoked, it will be responsible for triggering multiple worker functions, passing them the needed data to do their jobs. The key to this entire architecture is that the triggering of the worker processes occurs in such a way that they all run in parallel, or as close to parallel as possible.

Synchronous versus asynchronous invocation

The sole job of the entry point function is to initiate the fan-out and distribute work to multiple sub-functions. With this design, it's important to remember our goal, to parallelize the workload such that all of the worker functions are running in parallel. Just as our naive implementation with a for loop works synchronously, it's entirely possible to attempt to build an architecture as pictured above, but wind up with one which is synchronous. How can this happen?

Eventually, the entry point must make multiple calls to kick off the sub-tasks. For that, we'll use some form of looping. Using AWS as an example, the entry point can use the AWS APIs to invoke Lambda functions within that loop. The following code block demonstrates invoking a lambda function via the JavaScript AWS SDK:

```
const sizes = [128, 256, 1024];
const lambda = new aws.Lambda();

for (var i=0; i<sizes.length; i++) {
  var params = {
    FunctionName: 'fanout-ResizeImage',
    Payload: JSON.stringify({"size": sizes[i]})
  }

  lambda.invoke(params, function(error, data) {
    if (error) {
      callback(error)
    }
    else {
      callback(null, 'success')
    }
  });
}
```

It's safe to ignore much of the detail in the preceding code block. At a high level, our Node.js code iterates around an array of three items and invokes a named Lambda function each time. You may think that this code implements the architecture shown in the diagram above. However, running this, you'd quickly learn that this code operates entirely synchronously. That is, each iteration of the loop waits for a response to be returned from the `lambda.invoke` call. The reason for this is that, by default, Lambda invocation APIs assume a request type of request/response. More plainly, the default mode of operation is synchronous, where the client is expecting a return value from the invoked function. The good news is that this is trivial to fix by calling the `invoke` function with the correct parameter, which instructs it that we don't care about a return value. Merely add `InvocationType: "Event"` to the `params` and you're all done.

Resizing images in parallel

This example will be implemented in Node.js for no other reason than to change things from the Python code in previous chapters. There is a single dependency in this example, which we use for the image resizing, called `jimp`. I'll touch on some of the steps to get going with a new Node project using the Serverless Framework.

Setting up the project

Setting up a new Node.js project isn't any different from doing so with any other supported language. We'll tell serverless to use the `aws-nodejs` template and name our project `fanout`. The `-p` argument simply tells Serverless to place all of the generated code in the `serverless` directory, which is relative to the location where we execute this command. Consider the following code:

```
root@4b26ed909d56:/code# sls create -t aws-nodejs -p serverless -n fanout
```

Next, we'll add our single dependency for `jimp`. Here, I'm using `yarn`, but `npm` works fine as well:

```
root@4b26ed909d56:/code/serverless# yarn add jimp
yarn add v1.3.2
info No lockfile found.
[1/4] Resolving packages...
[2/4] Fetching packages...
[3/4] Linking dependencies...
```

```
[4/4] Building fresh packages...
success Saved lockfile.
success Saved 88 new dependencies.
....
Done in 4.33s.
```

Once all that is done, our code layout looks like the following:

```
$ tree -L 1 .
.
├── handler.js
├── node_modules
├── package.json
├── serverless.yml
└── yarn.lock
```

Setting up trigger and worker functions

Next, let's wire up the `trigger` function and define the `worker` function. As noted earlier, this entire process will begin upon uploading an image to S3. The Serverless Framework makes this type of wiring straightforward with the `events` section in `serverless.yml`:

```
functions:
  UploadImage:
    handler: handler.uploadImage
    events:
      - s3:
          bucket: brianz-image-resize-fanout
          event: s3:ObjectCreated:*
  ResizeImage:
    handler: handler.resizeImage
```

What this says is that the `uploadImage` function will be called whenever an object is created in the named S3 bucket. That's all there is to it. Again, this event could have been anything else supported in AWS, provided the trigger gives access to some image which needs resizing. If you're using a cloud provider other than AWS, you'll need to figure out which trigger makes sense for your platform.

You'll also notice the definition of the `ResizeImage` function. What's curious is that there are no `events` listed. That is because, in our case, the `uploadImage` function will act as the trigger, calling this Lambda function manually using `aws-sdk`.

Setting up permissions

As with all things AWS, we'll need to ensure IAM permissions are set up correctly. The UploadImage function will interact with a single AWS resource other than itself, and that is the ResizeImage function. For UploadImage to invoke ResizeImage, we need to grant it explicit permission.

Additionally, ResizeImage needs access to write data to the final resting place of the resized photos. We'll place these images in a different S3 bucket and again grant access via the iamRoleStatements section.

You can see both of these statements in the following code, along with other configurations in the full serverless.yml file:

```yaml
service: fanout

provider:
  name: aws
  runtime: nodejs4.3
  region: ${env:AWS_REGION}
  timeout: 30
  iamRoleStatements:
    - Effect: Allow
      Action:
        - lambda:InvokeFunction
      Resource: "arn:aws:lambda:${env:AWS_REGION}:*:function:fanout-
${opt:stage}-ResizeImage"
    - Effect: Allow
      Action:
        - s3:PutObject
      Resource:
        - "arn:aws:s3:::brianz-image-resize-fanout-results/*"

functions:
  UploadImage:
    handler: handler.uploadImage
    events:
      - s3:
          bucket: brianz-image-resize-fanout
          event: s3:ObjectCreated:*
  ResizeImage:
    handler: handler.resizeImage

plugins:
  - serverless-prune-plugin
```

From a security perspective, there is a slight imperfection in our IAM roles above since both functions are granted the same permissions. That is, `ResizeImage` is allowed to call itself, and `uploadImage` is allowed access to the results S3 bucket. Ideally, only the functions which need the permissions would be granted those permissions. It is possible to set up per-function IAM access using the Serverless Framework but it's a bit verbose and outside the scope of this book.

Implementing the application code

With the setup done, we can now focus on the application code. Let's take a look at the `uploadImage` function, as that is the gateway to the entire process.

We first need to initialize our two dependencies at the top of this `handler.js` file, as follows:

- The `aws-sdk`, which is automatically available in the Lambda runtime
- The `jimp` library for doing the image manipulation

Going from the top down, our `uploadImage` function defines a few things. First, our `params` object contains the base of the Lamda invocation parameters. Note here that we're using an `InvocationType` of `"Event"`, which is extremely important in order to get the asynchronous fan-out described earlier. Next, we'll hardcode a few image widths to which we'll resize the original image. `jimp` is capable of taking a single dimension (height or width) and automatically calculating the other dimension to retain the original aspect ratio.

The `uploadImage` function, when invoked, receives quite a bit of metadata about the invocation in the `event` parameter. In our case, the information about the uploaded images will be contained in this `event` object. All of that data ends up in an array of `Records`. In reality, there should only be a single record to deal with. Just to be safe, we'll continue working as if there are a variable number of items in here and grab them all.

Finally, this function will iterate around the array of different sizes and invoke the appropriate callback as many times, with a slightly different payload. The list of `S3Objects` is the same for each iteration, but the size field for each `resizeImage` invocation will be different. The following code block shows the full implementation of the `uploadImage` function, which invokes the `ResizeImage` Lambda function asynchronously:

```
'use strict';

const aws = require('aws-sdk');
```

```
const Jimp = require("jimp");


module.exports.uploadImage = (event, context, callback) => {
  var params = {
    FunctionName: 'fanout-dev-ResizeImage'
    , InvocationType: "Event"
  }

  var sizes = [128, 256, 1024];

  const s3Objects = event['Records'].map(function(r) {
    return r["s3"]
  })

  const lambda = new aws.Lambda({
    region: 'us-west-2'
  });

  for (var i=0; i<sizes.length; i++) {
    params['Payload'] = JSON.stringify({
      "size": sizes[i]
      , "s3Objects": s3Objects
    });

    lambda.invoke(params, function(error, data) {
      if (error) {
        callback(error)
      } else {
        callback(null, 'success')
      }
    });
  }

};
```

With that, we can turn our attention to the work on actually resizing the images. Just as in `uploadImage`, `resizeImage` receives a payload of data in the `event` parameter, which is an object type. Remember that the `S3Objects` attribute passed over to this function is an array of S3 images. It's safe to say that this will be an array of length one for this example.

As this function iterates around the list of `S3Objects`, it will extract the pertinent data needed for it to perform the following tasks:

1. Get the original image from S3
2. Resize the in-memory image contents

3. Write the resized image to a local buffer
4. Upload the resized image to the destination bucket with the updated name

The following code block shows the full implementation of the `resizeImage` function, which is responsible for downsizing an image:

```
module.exports.resizeImage = (event, context, callback) => {

  const size = event.size;
  const S3 = new aws.S3();

  event.s3Objects.map(function(s3Object) {
    var bucket = s3Object.bucket.name;
    var key = s3Object.object.key;
    var parts = key.split('.');
    var name = parts[0];
    var suffix = parts[1];

    function uploadToS3(err, buffer) {
      const keyName = name + "-" + size + "." + suffix
      var params = {
        Body: buffer,
        Bucket: bucket + '-results',
        Key: keyName
      }

      S3.putObject(params, function(err, data) {
        if ( err ) {
          callback(err);
        } else {
          console.log('successfully uploaded resized image: ' +
          keyName)
          callback(null, "success");
        }
      })
    }

    S3.getObject({Bucket: bucket, Key: key}, function(err, data) {
      if ( err ) {
        console.log('Error reading S3 item: ' + bucket + ' ' + key);
      } else {
        Jimp.read(data.Body, function(err, buffer) {
          buffer
            .resize(size, Jimp.AUTO)
            .getBuffer( Jimp.MIME_JPEG, uploadToS3 )
        })
      }
```

```
    });

    callback(null, "success");

  });

};
```

Testing our code

To test this, all that's needed is to upload an image to our target directory. I'll use one of my photos from the High Sierra in California, along with the AWS command-line interface. The original photo is 2,816 × 2,112 pixels:

```
$ aws s3 cp 1186218980_878902b096_o.jpg s3://brianz-image-resize-fanout/ --
acl public-read
upload: ./1186218980_878902b096_o.jpg to s3://brianz-image-resize-
fanout/1186218980_878902b096_o.jpg
```

Let's inspect the logs from the `ResizeImage` function. What we expect to see is three invocations right around the same time. Bear in mind that these may finish at entirely different times since the workload between them may vary; however, the starting times should be very close together. Looking at the **CloudWatch** log results, we can see what we're hoping for:

Success! Each one of these log streams corresponds to a unique invocation of `ResizeImage`. Additionally, the **Last Event Time** is precisely the same across all three invocations.

 In this case, each **Log Streams** corresponds to a single invocation, but that isn't always necessarily true. As more and more requests come in, CloudWatch will group Log statements into existing streams. Here, I started with no **Log Streams** at all for clarity.

It's possible to view the logs in the AWS console or use the `sls logs` command to see them all together. Unfortunately, the start times are not automatically added to the `CloudWatch`, `Log` statement when using the AWS API (which is what `sls` commands ultimately use). However, we can see the results from any of our `console.log` statements along with the ending times:

```
root@39152c09a5f4:/code/serverless# sls logs -f ResizeImage -s $ENV
START RequestId: 5cc66bc4-e53e-11e7-ba30-f5d23778d6cb
    Version: $LATEST
START RequestId: 5cc5f6f2-e53e-11e7-8ff7-c3f67f0d5aef
    Version: $LATEST
START RequestId: 5cc6e173-e53e-11e7-9de2-85f253c2cf2b
    Version: $LATEST

2017-12-20 04:29:34.608 (+00:00) 5cc6e173-e53e-11e7-9de2-85f253c2cf2b
   successfully uploaded resized image: 1186218980_878902b096_o.jpg-128.jpg
END RequestId: 5cc6e173-e53e-11e7-9de2-85f253c2cf2b
REPORT RequestId: 5cc6e173-e53e-11e7-9de2-85f253c2cf2b
```

```
    Duration: 6059.70 ms Billed Duration: 6100 ms
    Memory Size: 1024 MB Max Memory Used: 424 MB

2017-12-20 04:29:34.696 (+00:00) 5cc66bc4-e53e-11e7-ba30-f5d23778d6cb
    successfully uploaded resized image: 1186218980_878902b096_o.jpg-256.jpg
END RequestId: 5cc66bc4-e53e-11e7-ba30-f5d23778d6cb
REPORT RequestId: 5cc66bc4-e53e-11e7-ba30-f5d23778d6cb
    Duration: 6302.95 ms Billed Duration: 6400 ms
    Memory Size: 1024 MB Max Memory Used: 426 MB

2017-12-20 04:29:35.456 (+00:00) 5cc5f6f2-e53e-11e7-8ff7-c3f67f0d5aef
    successfully uploaded resized image: 1186218980_878902b096_o.jpg-1024.jpg
END RequestId: 5cc5f6f2-e53e-11e7-8ff7-c3f67f0d5aef
REPORT RequestId: 5cc5f6f2-e53e-11e7-8ff7-c3f67f0d5aef
    Duration: 6980.45 ms Billed Duration: 7000 ms
    Memory Size: 1024 MB Max Memory Used: 481 MB
```

These results also make sense. The smallest resizing job uses the least amount of memory and completes first. The largest resize job uses the most memory and finishes last. We need to acknowledge that the 128 px job starts early and gets a tiny head start. However, looking at the duration, it's also clear that the total execution time is higher when the resized file is bigger. I suspect this is due to the uploading to S3 and not the resizing process itself. Regardless, for this example, it's unimportant which takes longer and why. What is important is that we now have a system which receives a single input and invokes multiple worker processes in parallel. Had this work been done synchronously, the execution would have taken approximately 20 seconds, which is the sum of all three resize durations. Using the fan-out pattern, this is cut down to 7 seconds, which is the time it takes for the longest running task to complete.

Looking into the S3 bucket of the results, we can view the three new images with the new widths embedded in the name. Additionally, you can see the image sizes vary, where the smallest image has the smallest file size and the largest image the largest file size:

```
$ aws s3 ls s3://brianz-image-resize-fanout-results/1186218980_878902b096_o
2017-12-20 04:29:36 1027150 1186218980_878902b096_o-1024.jpg
2017-12-20 04:29:35 20795 1186218980_878902b096_o-128.jpg
2017-12-20 04:29:35 78093 1186218980_878902b096_o-256.jpg
```

Alternate Implementations

The preceding example is merely one, albeit common, example of how you can implement a fan-out pattern. There are many ways to turn one event or trigger into multiple parallel processes. Some options for this are specific to the cloud service you're using. Since the vast majority of my cloud experience is with AWS, I'll cover some alternative architectures. These may be portable to other cloud providers with corollary service offerings under different names.

Using notifications with subscriptions

My preceding example was controlled by a master receiver function, which was invoked on some trigger and then performed the work of calling the worker processes manually. One alternative is to replace the entry point function with a **Simple Notification Service (SNS)** topic. If you're unfamiliar with SNS, it's just what it sounds like—a system which, when triggered, notifies subscribers that something has happened.

Because our example was focused on transforming an image in multiple ways, it makes sense to set up a trigger when a new file is added. However, what happens when we want to start doing some processing when another type of event occurs? For example, a new user signs up on our website via their Facebook account, and we want to do the following:

- Send them a welcome email
- Set up their account
- Pull their Facebook social graph

This workflow is all made up, but the main idea is the same—a single event results in multiple jobs, which may operate in parallel.

In cases like this, an event of interest would trigger an SNS notification on a particular topic. SNS payloads can contain whatever your application code decides to send. Downstream, zero or more subscribers may be listening to that topic and choose to do some work when a new notification arrives. On AWS, Lambda functions may be triggered by SNS notifications.

Our fan-out architecture looks slightly different if using SNS to trigger one or more Lambda workers:

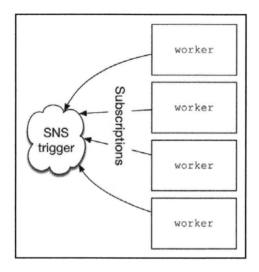

Now we're freed from the burden of keeping track of what worker processes need to be called when an interesting event occurs. With the SNS design, individual workers subscribe to the SNS topic and trigger upon receiving an SNS notification. It's important to note that each one of these workers is a unique Lambda function with separate application code. In case, where the parallel jobs are all performing disparate tasks, there is no problem, since these would always need to be separated out and managed as unique functions. This design fits very nicely when the work to be parallelized can occur based on a singular event, but where each job is unique and can stand alone. Crawling a user's Facebook social graph and inserting some records in your database are entirely separable. For that reason, this architecture is an excellent choice. When a new job needs to run based on the same event, the work involves implementing the application code and subscribing to the existing SNS topic.

This model doesn't work very well if all of the workers are performing the same task. The reason for this is that an SNS trigger occurs on a single topic and delivers the same payload to all subscribers. In the image resize example, the `UploadImage` function invoked `ResizeImage` three times with three different payloads. If we had built the image resize example with the SNS design, each resizing worker would need to be its own independently managed Lambda function with the knowledge of what size to use when resizing images. To be more clear, there would be three different Lambda functions which corresponded to the three different image sizes we wanted to resize:

- `ResizeImage256`
- `ResizeImage512`
- `ResizeImage1024`

If we wanted to add a new image size, it would mean implementing a new function. That rapidly becomes unwieldy, and problems such as this aren't a good fit for this design.

Using notifications with queues

Another take on this is to use an SNS notification to deliver to multiple queues. When an SNS event is triggered, that notification takes place fairly quickly (a few seconds, at most). If there are 100 subscribers attached to that topic, all 100 subscribers will wake up and start working in parallel. That behavior may be exactly what you need in certain scenarios. However, in those cases where you may not want your system to operate at full capacity, it's possible to deliver SNS data to one or more **Simple Queuing Service (SQS)** queues:

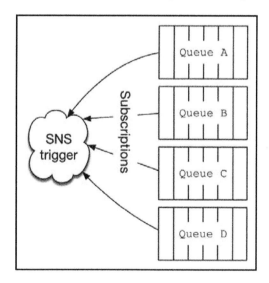

Here, the subscribers to an SNS topic are SQS queues rather than Lamba functions. This sort of design may work well when you don't necessarily want, or need to keep up with, a high volume of events. By throwing data on queues, it's easier to control the consumption rate of the data.

SQS behaves as one would expect a queue to act; that is, data placed into the queue remains in the queue until some process comes along and consumes it, finally marking it as consumed. This pattern would be a great design to protect some backing service such as a relational database. Take the case where a high number of transactions arrives all at once and they ultimately need to be written to a database. Using the previous example, this could result in an equally high number of database writes since there is nothing to slow down the workers being invoked once the SNS event is triggered. To buffer that work, the SNS notifications trigger writes to the SQS queues, which result in all of the data queuing up for future processing. Workers process then poll the queues at some acceptable and known rate so as not to overwhelm the database either saturating the number of open connections or putting too much load on it.

Summary

This chapter introduced the fan-out pattern and discussed its overall merits and basic architecture when using a serverless platform. We discussed, in detail, the implementation of an example serverless application, which created multiple resized images in parallel using this pattern. In this example, we also learned the basics of deploying a Node.js application using the Serverless Framework on top of AWS. We also discussed different implementations of the fan-out pattern using different AWS services and when those alternative designs may be suitable.

Readers should understand the fan-out pattern well and be ready to use this pattern in future chapters in this book as part of more complex patterns.

Next, we'll work on processing data using queues and the messaging pattern.

6
Asynchronous Processing with the Messaging Pattern

In the last chapter, we discussed the Fan-out Pattern, which we can implement using different strategies. At the end of that section, we reviewed an implementation of the Fan-out Pattern, which used AWS's Simple Queuing Service (SQS) as a destination for an event trigger. Queuing systems such as SQS provide a level of safety and security because they're intended to be a mostly durable persistent store where data lives until some process has the chance to pull it out, perform some work, and delete the item. If a downstream worker processes a crash entirely and processing stops for some time, queues merely back up, drastically reducing the risk of data loss. If a worker process runs into some unrecoverable problem in the middle of processing, queue items will typically be left on the queue to be retried by another processor in the future.

In this chapter, we will cover using queues as messaging systems to glue together multiple serverless components. Readers can already be familiar with queuing systems such as RabbitMQ, ActiveMQ, or SQS. We will learn how to pass messages between serverless systems using queues to provide durable and fault-tolerant distributed systems for data-heavy applications.

At the end of this chapter, you can expect to understand the following topics:

- What queuing systems are available and make sense in a serverless architecture
- Options for processing messages using serverless functions (polling and fan-out)
- Differences between queues and streaming systems and when to use one over the other
- Dead letter queues to ensure messages are never dropped
- Using queues as a way of rate limiting

Basics of queuing systems

Queuing systems are by no means new in the world of software. Generally speaking, queues are one of the fundamental data structures most introductory computer science courses cover. Before going any further, let's briefly review the queue as a fundamental data structure in computer science.

Simply put, a queue is a collection of items where new items are pushed onto the back and pulled off the front. Consider that we're all waiting in line for a movie. Provided people follow the rules and don't line up out of order, you've waited in a queue (which is, of course, the reason British English uses *queue*, which is more accurate than the U.S. term *line*). Formally, we can define a queue as a collection of items that have the property of first-in-first-out (FIFO). The primary operators of a queue data type are `enqueue` and `dequeue`. These operators add new items to the back of the queue and pop items off the front, respectively.

In software, queueing systems such as RabbitMQ and the like are commonly used to deal with asynchronous processing. A triggered event can mean that your system needs to perform some recalculations or data processing that doesn't need to occur in real time. Rather than having a user sit and wait until they click a button, an application will place metadata into a queue that contains enough information for a downstream worker process to do its job. These worker processes' sole responsibility is to sit and wait until a new item arrives and then carry out some computation. As messages show up in the queue, workers pluck off those messages, do their work, and return for more. This architecture has multiple benefits:

- **Durability**: Provided clients write data to the queue successfully and the queuing system is healthy, messages will persist in the queue until there is enough computing power available to pull them off, process, and finally remove them.
- **Scalability**: Most queuing architectures are parallelizable, meaning multiple workers can pull messages from a queue and process individual items in parallel. To operate with more throughput, we can add more workers into the system, which results in faster processing through greater parallelism.
- **Predictable load:** Often, worker processes will need to read and/or write data from/to a database. When the load is exceptionally high, the queue can serve as a buffer between the processing tasks and database. To limit pressure on a database we can scale the number of worker processes such that the parallelism is as high as possible, but not so much we overwhelm the database with an inordinate amount of reads or writes.

Readers should note that they can implement a Messaging Pattern with either a queue or streaming system. In this chapter, we focus on queues but later discuss the merits of stream systems and the differences between the two types of message broker. In subsequent chapters, we will work through the details of streaming systems.

One of the most dangerous spots to be in is when all the incredible benefits of a queue are in place, only to have the actual queue server (RabbitMQ and so on) running as a single node. I have worked at multiple companies that have relied quite heavily on RabbitMQ as the queueing backbone, running very high business-critical workloads from it. However, we ran these RabbitMQ deployments as a single EC2 instance with lots of computing capacity. Inevitably, when an individual instance runs into problems or for some reason dies, the entire system falls apart, resulting in lost messages, failing clients who attempt to write the queue and error out, and an all-around bad day.

Choosing a queue service

The good news today is that multiple cloud providers now offer queuing systems as a service. In the following examples, we'll use SQS from AWS. While I haven't worked with them directly, Google Compute Cloud has Task Queue, and Azure has Queue Storage. Undoubtedly, other cloud providers offer similar services. When evaluating hosted queuing services, there are several factors to consider:

- What type of data fetching model is supported, pull or push?
- What is the maximum lifetime of messages or the maximum queue depth?
- What happens with messages that consistently fail? Is there a dead-letter queue option?
- Is there a guarantee of exactly-once delivery, or can messages be delivered multiple times?
- Is ordering guaranteed, or can messages arrive out of order relative to the order from which they were sent?

Answers to these questions will vary by provider and by service offering for a given cloud provider. SQS, for example, comes in two flavors: Standard Queues and FIFO Queues. Which one you'll pick when building on top of AWS will come down to your particular use case. If building with a different cloud provider, you'll need to dig into their documentation to fully understand the behavior and semantics of whatever queueing service you're using.

Queues versus streams

You can think of a queue as a broker of messages. Some data producer will place messages onto the queue, and some data consumer will read those messages. The queue simply brokers that exchange of message passing. Stream processing systems provide similar functionality, but with much different behavior, features, and applications. I'll present a brief discussion of the differences between queues and streams for the sake of clarity.

Apache Kafka is a very popular stream processing system in widespread use, of which you can have heard. Today, cloud providers have come out with hosted stream processing systems:

- **Azure**: Event Hubs
- **AWS**: Kinesis
- **Google Compute Cloud**: Cloud Dataflow

So, what exactly is a stream processing system as opposed to a queueing system? To my mind, the most significant and most easily understood difference is the way in which items are processed or delivered. In a queuing system, messages that arrive in the queue are typically processed once, by a single process. There are of course exceptions to this rule, but in all systems I've worked on that use a queue, the *happy path* was designed such that a single message would be read and processed once.

Streaming systems, on the other hand, can be thought of as a collection of records where old records eventually expire off the back (the oldest expiring first), and new records are added to the front. Rather than being processed and removed, messages sit there, without knowledge of who is reading them and without being deleted by consumers. Data consumers are responsible for keeping track of their position within the stream using an offset value. The streaming service itself is responsible for retaining the messages, generally with some configurable expiration period:

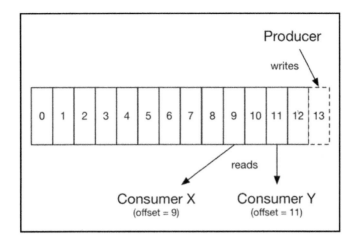

It is possible to have multiple consumers reading and processing the same message when using a streaming system. For example, one consumer can be reading items on the stream and calculating a running average of some metric, while another consumer can be reading the same messages and calculating the standard deviation. In a queuing system, this wouldn't be possible without duplicating messages across different queues or implementing some logic or heuristic to remove messages only after all consumers have done their job. Either way, a queue would not be a good fit for such a problem whereas streaming systems are purpose-built just for this.

Another exciting feature of streaming systems is that new consumers who come online can start at the back of the stream and work forward. For example, if a stream holds one week's worth of data, any new system that starts will be able to go back seven days and begin its processing from there. Because consumers keep track of their location or offset within the stream, they can pick up where they left off in the case of failure.

Technically speaking, you can implement the Messaging Pattern with a queue or a stream, and the choice depends on the problem at hand. We'll look at AWS Kinesis and discuss streaming systems in later chapters. For now, we'll focus on using queues and specifically SQS for the example application. In my mind, a Message Pattern at its core entails separating the communication between different system via some message broker, such as a queue or streaming system.

Asynchronous processing of Twitter streams

Twitter is an excellent source of random data. Given the volume and variety of data, we can readily come up with example (and real) problems to solve. In our case, we're going to build a serverless processing system by sipping off the public twitter stream. Our example system will have the following workflow:

1. Read a tweet with cat or dog images from the Twitter firehose
2. Place messages on an SQS queue.
3. Worker processes will read those image URLs off the queue and perform image recognition.

While this example can be a bit contrived, the concepts demonstrated are true to life. We'll use the AWS Rekognition service to perform image recognition and labeling of any cat or dog images we find. Rekognition is quite fast at what it does, but it's easy to imagine processing images with a much slower service. In that case, adding items onto a queue and processing them at our leisure with one or more worker processes would allow us to scale out to achieve a higher processing rate.

You can find all code in this chapter at `https://github.com/brianz/serverless-design-patterns/tree/master/ch6`.

System architecture

The system architecture for our image analysis example is quite simple. Ingestion of tweets will begin using a stream listener for the Twitter API via the Python `tweepy` library, `https://github.com/tweepy/tweepy`. This listener will filter out only specific tweets on our behalf. From there, the listener will place messages onto an SQS queue. Once it delivers messages to the queue, the job of our stream listener is complete. With this type of design, we realize a real separation of concerns. If we enumerated the things our stream listener cares about, the list would be quite short:

- Twitter access
- Some business logic as to what types of data to extract from tweets
- Which queue to place the extracted tweet information in

That is it. Once the stream listener performs the last step of adding items onto the queue, it neither cares about nor is affected by, any downstream processing or lack thereof.

From there, worker processes will pull images off the queue and perform their bit of work, ultimately calling AWS Rekognition and storing the results in DynamoDB for future review. Our example will use a classifier processor, which will run with a single level of parallelism. That is, at any given time there will only be a single classifier process running. However, there would be very few changes if we wished to scale this out and operate multiple classifiers at the same time, increasing our parallelism and hence the overall throughput of the system.

Again, with this design, the classifier's job is much simpler than if we implemented all of this work as a single process. Classifiers also care about a small number of items to perform their work:

- Which queue to get data from
- A small bit of business logic to perform the image classification
- Where to put the results

Our classifier neither knows nor cares how data arrived in the queue. All that matters from the classifier's perspective is that data comes with the correct format (which is quite simple) and that is has access to the resources it needs to perform its job.

With a queue acting as the broker between data producer (stream listener) and data consumer (classifier), we have a reasonably good level of durability. If our listener dies (which it will by design, as you'll see shortly) or if our classifiers die, SQS will hold onto our data, ensuring we can get to it and process it when our systems are back to full health. Also, we'd be able to scale this up as needed, adding more classifiers in the event that the stream listener produced more messages than a single classifier could keep up:

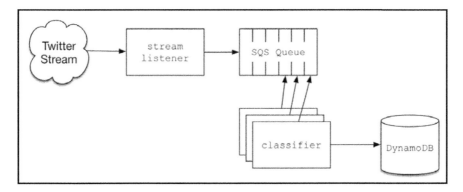

Messages are placed onto an SQS queue by a stream listener process, which is implemented as an AWS Lambda function and runs on a schedule. A single classifier Lambda function also runs on a schedule and is responsible for pulling messages from the queue, classifying them with AWS Rekognition and finally storing results in DynamoDB.

Furthermore, this design allows for a level of flexibility that would be difficult otherwise. Our example is processing tweets tagged with #cat or #dog and a few other related hashtags. We could also modify our stream processor to grab a more extensive set of tweets, perhaps directed at @realDonaldTrump. Those tweets could be directed to an entirely different queue, which would be processed separated and completely different. Since the volume of @realDonalTrump tweets is much higher than #cat and #dog tweets, separating them out and handling them differently would be an excellent idea from a systems architecture perspective.

Data producer

Most of the complexities in this code revolve around the Twitter API, which I won't go into in detail. I haven't worked with the Twitter API much myself, but the tweepy GitHub page and website have plenty of resources and example code to get you started, which is just what I followed to get this working. The following code is the entry point to the entire process, which begins reading the public Twitter stream for tweets related to cats or dogs and placing a subset of each tweet onto the SQS queue:

```python
import os
import tweepy

from .queue import publish_tweet

consumer_key = os.environ['TWITTER_CONSUMER_KEY']
consumer_secret = os.environ['TWITTER_CONSUMER_SECRET']

access_token = os.environ['TWITTER_ACCESS_TOKEN']
access_token_secret = os.environ['TWITTER_ACCESS_SECRET']


class PhotoStreamListener(tweepy.StreamListener):

    def _get_media_urls(self, media):
        if not media:
            return []

        return [m['media_url_https'] for m in media if m['type'] ==
        'photo']
```

```python
    def _get_hashtags(self, container):
        hashtags = [h['text'] for h in container.get('hashtags', ())]
        return [h for h in hashtags if '#' + h in self.tags]

    def on_status(self, tweet):
        container = tweet._json

        entities = container.get('entities', {}).get('media')
        extended_entities = container.get('extended_entities',
        {}).get('media')
        extended_tweet = container.get('extended_tweet',
        {}).get('entities', {}).get('media')

        all_urls = set()
        for media in (entities, extended_entities, extended_tweet):
            urls = self._get_media_urls(media)
            all_urls.update(set(urls))

        hashtags = self._get_hashtags(container.get('entities', {}))

        if all_urls:
            for url in all_urls:
                publish_tweet({
                    'text': tweet.text,
                    'url': url,
                    'hashtags': hashtags,
                })

    @staticmethod
    def start(tags=None):
        tags = tags or ['#dog', '#dogs', '#puppy', '#cat', '#kitty',
        '#lolcat', '#kitten']

        auth = tweepy.OAuthHandler(consumer_key, consumer_secret)
        auth.set_access_token(access_token, access_token_secret)

        api = tweepy.API(auth)

        listener = PhotoStreamListener()
        listener.tags = tags
        stream = tweepy.Stream(auth=api.auth, listener=listener)
        try:
            stream.filter(track=tags)
        except Exception as e:
            print 'Shutting down'
            print e
```

Let's begin by looking at the start function, which does what you'd expect. Once the listener class is instantiated and begins running, it will operate as a long-lived daemon process invoking the on_status function whenever it encounters a tweet. Since we are only interested in certain types of message, I'll pass a list of tags to the filter function.

All of our application logic is wrapped up in the on_status method. Tweets are a reasonably elaborate data structure, and the actual image URLs we're interested in can live in multiple locations. As a Twitter API novice, I'm not entirely sure of the exact logic to look for image URLs, but the little bit of logic in on_status seems to get enough images for our example. After grabbing as many image URLs as we can along with some extracted hashtags, we will publish that data structure to our SQS queue using our publish_tweet wrapper function. Details on publish_tweet can be found in the following queue-specific code block. It's not complex at all, and the only really important bit is to understand what exactly ends up on the queue. In this case, we're placing a Python dictionary onto SQS, which ultimately gets serialized as a JSON record. This record contains the original tweet text, a URL for the cat or dog image, and any hashtags embedded in the tweet:

```
publish_tweet({
    'text': tweet.text,
    'url': url,
    'hashtags': hashtags,
})
```

Mimicking daemon processes with serverless functions

By definition, serverless functions are short-lived and have a maximum lifetime before your platform of choice kills them. At the time of writing, the current limitation for an AWS Lambda function is 300 seconds (5 minutes) and the default 6 seconds. Our example relies on a long-lived process that is continually reading from the Twitter stream and publishing those results to the queue. How then can we accomplish this long-lived behavior with an inherently short-lived system?

To mimic a constantly-running process, we can take advantage of the scheduled invocation of Lambda functions. Other cloud providers should provide similar functionality. In short, we can use the maximum lifetime of Lambda functions to our advantage. The trick here is to set the timeout value of our Lambda function to 58 seconds, which is just below the scheduled invocation rate of 60 seconds.

Since that code will run indefinitely, we can rely on AWS killing the Lambda function after 58 seconds. After a running `Firehose` Lambda function is killed, we know another one will start up within a second or two, which results in a continually running `Firehose` process.

There is a chance that there will be one or two seconds when two instances of firehose processing run concurrently. In this case, that's not a concern since the data consumer can handle duplicate data elegantly by merely ignoring duplicates. If you plan on using the same pattern, it's essential to ensure your data consumer can deal with duplicates and is idempotent with its computation and processing. This pattern may not be applicable for all problems, but it works well for this and similar systems:

```
service: twitter-stream

provider:
  name: aws
  runtime: python2.7
  memorySize: 128
  region: ${env:AWS_REGION}
  iamRoleStatements:
    - Effect: Allow
      Action:
        - sqs:*
      Resource:
"arn:aws:sqs:${env:AWS_REGION}:*:${env:ENV}TwitterFirehoseQueue"
    - Effect: Allow
      Action:
        - rekognition:DetectLabels
      Resource: "*"
    - Effect: "Allow"
      Action:
        - "dynamodb:*"
      Resource:
"arn:aws:dynamodb:${env:AWS_REGION}:*:table/${env:DYNAMODB_RESULTS_TABL
E_NAME}"
  environment:
    TWITTER_ACCESS_SECRET: ${env:TWITTER_ACCESS_SECRET}
    TWITTER_ACCESS_TOKEN: ${env:TWITTER_ACCESS_TOKEN}
    TWITTER_CONSUMER_KEY: ${env:TWITTER_CONSUMER_KEY}
    TWITTER_CONSUMER_SECRET: ${env:TWITTER_CONSUMER_SECRET}
    TWITTER_STREAM_QUEUE_NAME: ${env:ENV}TwitterFirehoseQueue
    DYNAMODB_RESULTS_TABLE_NAME: ${env:DYNAMODB_RESULTS_TABLE_NAME}

package:
  exclude:
    - .git/**
    - __pycache__/**
```

```
    - "**/__pycache__/**"
    - "*.pyc"
    - "*.swp"

resources:
  Resources:
    FirehoseSQS:
      Type: AWS::SQS::Queue
      Properties:
        QueueName: ${env:ENV}TwitterFirehoseQueue
        VisibilityTimeout: 30
    DynamoResultsTable:
      Type: AWS::DynamoDB::Table
      Properties:
        TableName: ${env:DYNAMODB_RESULTS_TABLE_NAME}
        AttributeDefinitions:
          - AttributeName: url
            AttributeType: S
        KeySchema:
          - AttributeName: url
            KeyType: HASH
        ProvisionedThroughput:
          ReadCapacityUnits: ${env:DYNAMODB_TABLE_READ_IOPS}
          WriteCapacityUnits: ${env:DYNAMODB_TABLE_WRITE_IOPS}

functions:
  Firehose:
    handler: handler.firehose
    timeout: 58
    events:
      - schedule: rate(1 minute)
  Classify:
    handler: handler.classify
    timeout: 58
    events:
      - schedule: rate(1 minute)
```

Data consumers

If you've worked with RabbitMQ or other queuing systems, you can be used to registering workers on specific queues or topics where those listeners/workers get notified when messages of interest arrive. With SQS, the model is entirely different. SQS is a purely poll-based system; that is, any code that is interested in reading data from a queue needs to poll using the appropriate AWS APIs. Additionally, application code must explicitly delete messages from the queue once it has completed its processing.

Some APIs for other queuing systems will automatically `ack` a message provided no exception occurs, resulting in the removal of those message from the queue. It's imperative to remember to delete messages from an SQS queue even if no processing should occur.

Just as the `Firehose` function executes on a one-minute interval, so too will our `Classify` process. When this function runs, it starts by pulling batches of records from the SQS queue in quantities of 10. You can see in the following that there is an infinite loop with the `while True:` statement. Again, once this loop starts, it will run until the Lambda itself terminates it according to our 58-second timeout. If there aren't any messages available for processing, everything just shuts down. This technique is more straightforward to implement and less expensive than dealing with the process sleeping. By merely quitting we can rely on the next run to pick up the next batch of work and don't need to waste CPU cycles doing anything but wait for messages to arrive:

```python
import boto3
import json
import os
import urllib2

from decimal import Decimal

TWITTER_STREAM_QUEUE_NAME = os.environ['TWITTER_STREAM_QUEUE_NAME']

from .storage import ClassiferResults

_sqs_client = None
_s3_client = None
_sqs_url = None


def get_sqs_client():
    global _sqs_client
    if _sqs_client is None:
        _sqs_client = boto3.client('sqs')
    return _sqs_client


def get_queue_url():
    global _sqs_url
    if _sqs_url is None:
        client = get_sqs_client()
        response =
        client.get_queue_url(QueueName=TWITTER_STREAM_QUEUE_NAME)
        _sqs_url = response['QueueUrl']
    return _sqs_url
```

```
def publish_tweet(payload):
    msg = json.dumps(payload)
    client = get_sqs_client()
    sqs_url = get_queue_url()

    return client.send_message(
            QueueUrl=sqs_url,
            MessageBody=msg)


def classify_photos():
    rekognition = boto3.client('rekognition')
    sqs = get_sqs_client()
    sqs_url = get_queue_url()

    while True:
        response = sqs.receive_message(
            QueueUrl=sqs_url,
            MaxNumberOfMessages=10,
        )
        messages = response.get('Messages')
        if not messages:
            break

        for msg in messages:
            receipt = msg['ReceiptHandle']
            body = json.loads(msg['Body'])

            url = body['url']

            # first check if we already have this image
            classifier_store = ClassiferResults(url=url)
            if classifier_store.exists:
                print 'Deleting queue item due to duplicate image'
                sqs.delete_message(QueueUrl=sqs_url,
                ReceiptHandle=receipt)
                continue

            image_response = urllib2.urlopen(url)
            results = rekognition.detect_labels(Image={'Bytes':
            image_response.read()})

            scores = [{
                'Confidence': Decimal(l['Confidence']),
                'Name': l['Name'],
            } for l in results['Labels']]

            classifier_store.upsert(
```

```
        text=body['text'],
        hashtags=body['hashtags'],
        scores=scores,
        labels=[l['Name'] for l in results['Labels']],
    )

    sqs.delete_message(QueueUrl=sqs_url, ReceiptHandle=receipt)
```

After the `classify_photos` function finds some messages, processing them isn't very complicated. With tweets, there is a good chance our classifier will encounter duplicate photos. This job will store results in DynamoDB, so the first step is to check whether that URL already exists. Our DynamoDB table will use the URL as the partition key, which is analogous to a simple primary key in a relational database. This DynamoDB schema means that the URL must be unique. If we've already stored a particular URL, we won't do any more processing. Still, we need to remember to delete the message from the queue. Without that step, worker processes would repeatedly process a queue item, resulting in a never empty queue.

For any new URLs, we'll download the image and throw it over to the AWS Rekognition service to get a listing of labels and associated scores. If you're unfamiliar with Rekognition, it's quite a fantastic service. Rekognition provides several impressive features such as facial recognition. We'll be using the image detection or *labeling* feature, which will detect objects in a given image with a corresponding score:

As an example, this image of a cat results in the following `Labels` from Rekognition:

```
{
    "Labels": [
        {
            "Name": "Animal",
            "Confidence": 86.34986877441406
        },
        {
            "Name": "Cat",
            "Confidence": 86.34986877441406
        },
        {
            "Name": "Kitten",
            "Confidence": 86.34986877441406
        },
        {
            "Name": "Mammal",
            "Confidence": 86.34986877441406
        },
        {
            "Name": "Pet",
            "Confidence": 86.34986877441406
        },
        {
            "Name": "Manx",
            "Confidence": 82.7002182006836
        },
        {
            "Name": "Asleep",
            "Confidence": 54.48805618286133
        },
        {
            "Name": "Siamese",
            "Confidence": 52.179630279541016
        }
    ]
}
```

So, our worker process will fetch pictures embedded in tweets and hand them off to Rekognition for labeling. Once Rekognition finishes its work, the worker process will store the scores and other data about the image and tweet in DynamoDB.

Viewing results

In this example, we don't have a custom user interface to view results, so the DynamoDB console will have to do. As we can see in the following screenshot, I'm storing image URLs along with any embedded hashtags from the original tweet as well as the detected labels and scores from the Rekognition query:

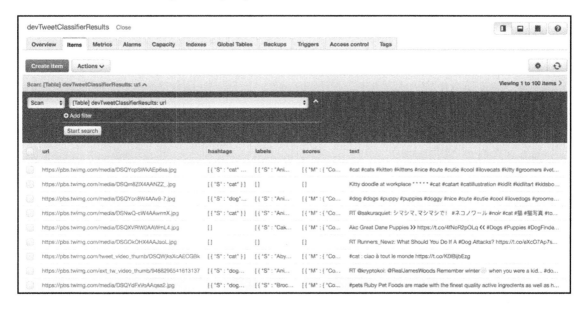

Using the DynamoDB API, let's take a look at one of the records in detail using Python's `boto3` library from Amazon:

```
>> import boto3
>>> url = 'https://pbs.twimg.com/media/DSQYcgMWAAAwfXf.jpg'
>>> dynamo = boto3.resource('dynamodb')
>>> table = dynamo.Table('devTweetClassifierResults')
>>> table.get_item(Key={'url': url})
{u'hashtags': [u'cat', u'kitten', u'kitty'],
 u'labels': [u'Animal', u'Pet', u'Cat', u'Mammal', u'Manx'],
 u'scores': [{u'Confidence': Decimal('86.49568939208984375'),
              u'Name': u'Animal'},
             {u'Confidence': Decimal('86.49568939208984375'),
              u'Name': u'Pet'},
             {u'Confidence': Decimal('79.18183135986328125'),
              u'Name': u'Cat'},
             {u'Confidence': Decimal('79.18183135986328125'),
              u'Name': u'Mammal'},
             {u'Confidence': Decimal('79.18183135986328125'),
```

```
                    u'Name': u'Manx'}],
  u'text': u'#cat #cats #kitten #kittens #nice #cute #cutie #cool #ilovecats
#kitty #groomers #vets #photooftheday #mycat\u2026
https://t.co/YXrs0JFb1d',
  u'url': u'https://pbs.twimg.com/media/DSQYcgMWAAAwfXf.jpg'}
```

With that, we have a reasonably sophisticated system with very few lines of application code. Most importantly and keeping this in context, every single system we've leveraged is entirely managed. Amazon will do the hard work of maintaining and scaling Lambda, SQS, and DynamoDB on our behalf. There are some tricks and essential details about managing DynamoDB read and write capacity and I encourage you to read up on that on your own.

Alternate Implementations

Our example application is quite robust and can handle quite a bit of load and traffic with few to no changes. As easy as this pattern is to understand, implement, and run, it's not a silver bullet. You will likely require different implementations of this Messaging Pattern in your scenarios. We'll review a few alternative applications of the same pattern, which uses a queue as a message broker between disparate systems.

Using the Fan-out and Messaging Patterns together

Earlier, during the explanation of our system architecture, I briefly discussed the possibility of fanning out messages from the stream listener to multiple queues. A design such as this would be useful when there are different types of workload to be performed from a single data producer. The following example architecture shows a system made up of an individual Twitter stream data producer that fans out messages to multiple queues based on the payload:

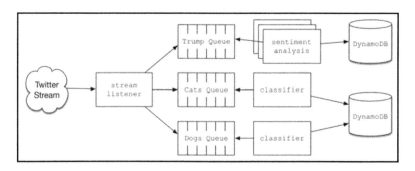

For this example, assume we're interested in processing a more extensive range of tweets. This system will still classify dog and cat images as before; however, this time we can split the processing apart more granularly by using separate queues for cat images and dog images. We can not be able to warrant this split in processing at the beginning, but it will allow us to treat and scale those systems separately.

A better example is the splitting of `@realDonaldTrump` tweets into an entirely different processing pipeline using a dedicated queue. The volume on this queue would be much higher than cat and dog images. Likely, we'd want to be running multiple concurrent workers to process this higher amount. Additionally, we could do something completely different from the labeling of images, such as running sentiment analysis on those tweets. Even in cases where the sentiment analysis was underprovisioned and got behind, we could feel confident knowing that any message on the queue could eventually be processed either by adding more worker processes or by an eventual slowdown of new messages from the data producer.

Using a queue as a rate-limiter

Many public APIs have rate limits. If you are attempting to pull down any substantial amount of data using a particular API that requires many API calls, you'll undoubtedly need to work around those rate limits and find a way to get to your data as fast as possible without exceeding your request quota. In cases such as this, a queue architecture can help out:

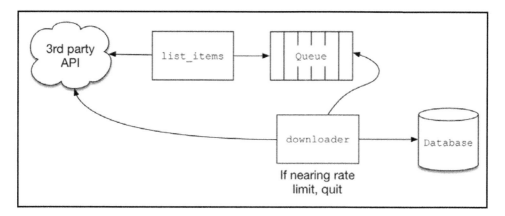

I have personally implemented this exact pattern with great success. Here, a third-party API provides an endpoint to /items. The actual data being retrieved is of little importance to explain the details. Here, the challenge is that we can only fetch the required details of these items by making another API call to an /items/${id} endpoint. When there are hundreds or thousands of things to download, which each require a separate API call (or more), we need to be careful to stay below the rate limit threshold. Typically, we would prefer that the system also runs as quickly as possible, so the overall process of retrieving item details doesn't take days or weeks.

With such constraints, we can use a queue and inspection of our consumption rate limit to download items as fast as possible while also staying within the bounds of our allotted rate limit. The trick here is to break up the work of producing objects for download from the act of downloading those objects. For the sake of this example, assume the /items endpoint retrieved up to 500 items at a time, where each element has a structure that includes a unique numeric id along with some metadata. Our goal of retrieving the entire view of each item requires another API call to /item/${id}. The data producer would make a single call to the /items endpoint and place messages onto the queue for each item that needs to be downloaded and stored. Each message on the queue would be somewhat generic, comprising a simple data structure such as {'url': 'https://some-domain.io/item/1234'}. This process could go as rapidly as it needed, since fetching an entire list of objects could realistically be done quite quickly and probably under whatever rate limit is imposed.

I put any intelligence about downloading item details and dealing with rate limiting into the downloader process. Just as with our cat and dog classifier, the downloader job is scheduled to wake up every minute and download as many messages as possible. Upon fetching the first item from the queue, the downloader will check the consumed rate limit which is provided by our third-party API via HTTP headers. There is no standard way of providing usage statistics to clients, but I've seen this type of data returned in the following header format: X-Ratelimit-Usage: 2142,3000. In this example, the API enforces a limit of 3,000 requests per unit time while the client has currently consumed 2,142 requests. If you do the math, 2,142 consumed units compared with a threshold of 3,000 equate to 71.4% usage.

After each API call, the downloader job checks its consumed API usage by doing this simple calculation. Once it nears some upper limit, the downloader can merely shut itself down and cease making API requests (perhaps when it gets above 90% usage). Of course, there must be a single API call made to inspect this usage. If the worker/downloader processes start up every two minutes, the worst-case scenario is that the system makes a single API call every two minutes. Only after some time has elapsed and the rate limits are reset (perhaps every 15 minutes) can the downloader start pulling items in bulk again. By using the same trick as our classifier example, it's trivial to have one or more downloader processing continually running by playing with the timeout value along with the scheduled invocation time.

Using a dead-letter queue

Under certain circumstances, worker processes can never successfully process a message sitting in a queue. Take for example our image classifier problem. The worker processes aren't responsible for much other than downloading an image, sending it to Rekognition, and storing those results in DynamoDB. However, what happens if, in between a tweet arriving in the queue and our processing of that tweet, a Twitter user deletes the original image or tweet. In this case, our classifier process would fail hard. Look for yourself, and you'll see there are no guards against an HTTP 404 response code from the image fetch.

A hard failure like this will result in the application code skipping the `sqs.delete_message` function altogether. After a configurable amount of time, that same message will be available on the queue to another worker who will encounter the same problem and fail in the same way. Without some protections in place, this cycle will repeat itself indefinitely.

It would be quite trivial to work around this case in the application code, since dealing with any non-200 HTTP response codes is quite easy and missing a few images isn't a significant problem. In more complicated applications where the failure scenarios cannot be as easy to foresee, setting up some fallback mechanism can be very helpful for debugging and for making the entire system more reliable. Specific queuing systems, including SQS, offer what is called a dead-letter queue.

A dead-letter queue is a separate queue where messages that cannot be successfully processed wind up. We can set up a dead-letter queue and configure our primary queue to place messages there if workers cannot successfully process messages after ten attempts. In that case, we guarantee the messages will eventually be removed from the primary queue either due to successful processing or by forceful removal due to 10 failures. A useful benefit of this is that we'll catch any problematic messages and can eventually inspect them and make changes to application code as needed. Since the dead-letter queue is a queue itself, we're still responsible for maintaining it and ensuring its health and size are kept in check.

Summary

In this chapter, we discussed the details of the Messaging Pattern and walked through a complete example using AWS SQS as a message broker. The example application comprised a Lambda function as the data producer, SQS as the message broker, and a Lambda function as the data consumer, which ultimately stored results in DynamoDB. We also discussed the difference between queues and streaming systems and reviewed their merits and use cases when one may be preferable over another. I also explained alternative architectures and implementations of the Messaging Pattern with specific problems and examples given for context.

At this point, readers should have a good understanding of how to break apart data-heavy serverless applications using queuing systems to provide scalability, fault tolerance, and reliability. I presented alternative architectures, which should give readers some insight into how they can structure their applications for improved decoupling and performance.

In the following chapter, we'll review another data-processing type of pattern which is useful in big data systems, the Lambda Pattern.

7

Data Processing Using the Lambda Pattern

This chapter describes the Lambda pattern, which is not to be confused with AWS Lambda functions. The Lambda architecture consists of two layers, typically used in data analytics processing. The two layers include a speed layer to calculate data in near-real time and a batch layer that processes vast amounts of historical data in batches.

Because serverless platforms allow us to scale horizontally very quickly, and since it's simple to store large amounts of data, the Lambda pattern is well suited for a serverless implementation. Lambda architectures are relatively new, coming onto the scene with the advent of big data processing and the desire to see the results of processing sooner than was previously available using batch systems such as Hadoop. This type of architecture or pattern is especially interesting since there are so many components involved in making it work, which we'll walk through using an example application that will calculate average prices for the cryptocurrencies Bitcoin and Ethereum.

By the end of this chapter, you can expect to have learned the following:

- A thorough understanding of the Lambda architecture and when it may be appropriate to use
- What tooling and options are available when designing a Lambda architecture in a serverless environment

- How to create a speed layer for processing a stream of cryptocurrency prices
- How to develop a batch layer for processing historical prices
- Alternate implementations and tooling when building a serverless Lambda architecture

Introducing the lambda architecture

To the best of my knowledge, Nathan Martz, author of Apache Storm, first introduced the lambda architecture in a 2011 blog post. You can read the post yourself at `http://nathanmarz.com/blog/how-to-beat-the-cap-theorem.html`. In this post, Nathan proposes a new type of system that can calculate historical views of large datasets alongside a real-time layer that can answer queries for real or near-real-time data. He labels these two layers the batch layer and the real-time layer.

The Lambda architecture was derived from trying to solve the problem of answering queries for data that is continuously updated. It's important to keep in mind the type of data we're dealing with here. Streaming data in this context are factual records. Some examples of streaming factual data are the following:

- The temperature at a given location at a given time
- An HTTP log record from a web server
- The price of Bitcoin from a given exchange at a given time

You can imagine the case where a temperature sensor is taking measurements in a given location and sending those readings somewhere every 5 seconds. If the temperature reading on January 31, 2018, at 12:00:00 was 75.4 °F, that fact should never change. A reading 5 seconds later may be 75.5 °F, but that does not nullify the prior reading. In this and other cases, we are working with an append-only data stream of facts.

Using our temperature analogy, imagine that we need to answer questions about this data such as the following:

- What was the average weekly temperature since 2010?
- What was the average monthly temperature since 2000?
- What were the daily high and low temperatures over the past year?
- What is the temperature trend over the past 2 hours?

Not only are we working with immutable data, but there is a time domain to consider as well in the queries to which we need to respond. If we had a naive implementation, we could store each piece of data in a relational database and perform queries on demand. There are 31,540,000 seconds in a year. If our system was uploading measurements every 5 seconds, that is 6,308,000 each year. Now, assume that we need to keep track of 10,000 different sensors around the world. This means our system would be adding 63,080,000,000 new records each year.

The initial challenge using a relational database would simply be finding a subset of those records for a particular location, for example, `SELECT * FROM temperatures where location_id = 1234`. Of course, we can undertake this type of query quickly using indexes, but there are significant limitations and trade-offs when dealing with billions or trillions of rows.

The second challenge would be performing calculations to get the right answer (that is, average temperature by week, high-low temperature each day). If our query was pulling data from 20 years ago until today, that would mean a lot of disk access and a significant load on the database, presuming the analytical query could be done in SQL.

Admittedly, there are systems that can deal with this level of scale, such as data warehouses or NoSQL data stores. However, data warehouses are not designed for real-time queries. NoSQL systems may be better at storing large amounts of data, but they lack flexibility or ability when it comes to running calculations on that data.

What is the solution when we have the level of scale of a data warehouse, a continually updated data stream and the requirement to serve queries in real time? This is where the Lambda pattern can help. Comprised of a batch layer and speed layer, the Lambda pattern is designed to solve this problem of responding to queries in real time, pulling data from both the batch layer and speed layer outputs.

Technically speaking, the view layer is a separate component of this architecture. As mentioned at the start of this chapter, there are many moving parts and components to a serverless implementation of the lambda pattern. For this reason, I won't be discussing the view layer in much detail so we can focus on the data portion of this pattern, which is more in tune with this chapter's theme. For a discussion of frontend applications in serverless systems, I'll refer you to Chapter 2, *A Three-Tier Web Application Using REST*.

The architecture is shown in the following diagram:

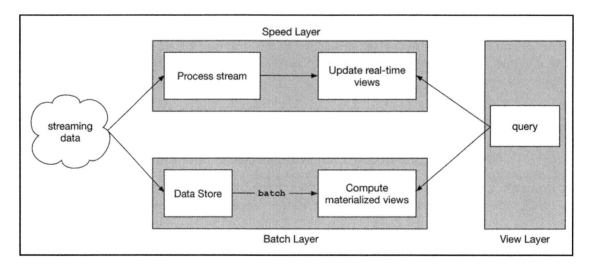

Batch layer

When the lambda architecture was proposed, Hadoop was already widely adopted and regarded as a proven technology. Hadoop is a linearly scalable system and can easily churn through terabytes of data in a reasonable amount of time to calculate nearly anything from your dataset. Here, *reasonable* may mean a job that runs for a few hours in the middle of the night so that new views of your data are ready first thing in the morning.

Using our temperature monitoring analogy, a day's worth of data will require a new batch job run if we need to calculate the average temperature in the month or year. Also, imagine we wanted to calculate trends day by day, month by month, or year by year. Whenever a new batch of daily temperatures is completed, our system would need to perform some work to calculate the pre-materialized views. By pre-calculating all of this data, any query would just look up the answer on demand without needing to calculate anything.

Speed layer

A batch layer by itself isn't anything new. The problem we're trying to solve here is answering queries quickly and up to date with a real-time view of our data stream. The magic with the Lambda pattern is the combination of the batch layer in conjunction with a speed layer.

The speed layer is a constantly updating system that processes new data from the data stream in real time. The calculations here will be the same as in the batch later, but it only works on a small subset of data as it arrives from the data stream. For example, to get the daily high temperature for a given location since 2015 in response to such a query, our system would do the following:

1. Fetch daily high temperatures from January 1, 2015, until yesterday from the batch layer
2. Fetch the high temperature from today from the speed layer
3. Merge the two datasets into one to present back to the user

Also note that in such a system, we could go even further. Our view layer could display the historical data in one area of the application and present the real-time information separately, which could be continually updated using a WebSocket connection or polling. By separating out these two layers, many options open up regarding application development and interaction.

Lambda serverless architecture

While the overall design and theme of a lambda architecture remain the same as a traditional system, there are variations and adaptations that we need to make. Perhaps more importantly, there are many different ways to implement this pattern using serverless systems or, at the very least, managed services.

Streaming data producers

Any system must start with data to process. On serverless platforms, there are multiple choices for streaming systems. Azure, Google Compute, and AWS all offer some form of streaming systems. I mentioned these in Chapter 6, *Asynchronous Processing with the Messaging Pattern,* when discussing the differences between queues and streams:

- **Azure**: Event Hubs
- **AWS**: Kinesis
- **Google Compute Cloud**: Cloud Dataflow

It's worth briefly touching on the topic of queues versus streams again. As mentioned in Chapter 6, *Asynchronous Processing with the Messaging Pattern,* one of the main differentiators is that queues are primarily designed for once-only processing. That is, once a message is pulled from a queue, no other consumer will see it. Data in a stream, on the other hand, has a given lifetime and cannot be removed by any consumer of that data. For example, a stream can set data to expire after 24 hours, or after 30 days. At any point in time, one or more readers can come along and begin reading data from the stream. It's up to the readers to keep track of where they are in the history of a stream. A new reader may start at the beginning of the stream, in the middle, or at the end.

Data storage

Since there are two distinct layers in this pattern, storage choices will likely be different since the two layers are drastically different in their data requirements. The batch layer requires extreme scalability and should perform well for a high number of concurrent reads during batch processing. The speed layer, on the other hand, doesn't need to store as much data but should be extremely fast for both reads and writes.

In many examples of this pattern, you'll see references to **Hadoop Filesystem (HDFS)** for storing historical data and NoSQL databases for real-time data. While it's near impossible to say what you should pick, it is possible to speak to some of your options.

Cloud storage systems such as AWS S3 or Google Cloud Storage were designed to fill a similar role as HDFS, that is, to store practically as much data as you need. The advantages of storing plain files on services such as this are that it's straightforward, requires almost no management, and is very durable. What I like about using flat or structured files is that it becomes possible to process the data later and store it in a different system such as a database. Also, there are a myriad of serverless or hosted systems that you can leverage that read data from these systems. Focusing only on AWS, the following systems can perform batch processing or analytical queries on S3 data:

- **Elastic MapReduce (EMR)**
- Athena
- Redshift

DynamoDB or other NoSQL are also options for historical data. Azure Cosmos DB and Google Bigtable are other services that I cannot speak to directly but that are options if you're building on top of those cloud providers.

 At least in the case of DynamoDB, special consideration should be made since read and write throughput needs to be carefully considered to maintain a workable system.

For the speed layer, there are also multiple tools you can use. DynamoDB is a viable choice since it's linearly scalable and you should have a fair idea of the read and write capacity needed. Managed Redis services such as AWS ElastiCache or Azure Redis Cache are also decent choices since Redis is exceptionally performant and the dataset is limited.

Computation in the speed layer

It makes sense that, since we're using serverless systems, our serverless functions will perform any computations necessary. Serverless functions are a natural choice, for what should be obvious reasons at this point. Running functions on demand or in response to new data arriving on our streams is incredibly simple. Additionally, FaaS allows us to scale horizontally.

In a lambda architecture, we may need to calculate many different metrics at the same time, from the same data stream. Doing this from a `single` serverless function could be possible. However, in the case where the computation is heavier, we may need to split out the computation into multiple functions, each calculating their own set of metrics from the same stream. Numerous readers allow us to scale out horizontally and provide the flexibility needed when data changes or new metrics need to be calculated.

While serverless functions are a natural choice and easily understood, there are other options. On AWS, it's possible to use Spark Streaming from within the EMR system. Spark Streaming is purpose-built for this type of workload. In the case that your data stream outgrows the limitations of cloud functions such as Lambda, moving to Spark Streaming is a good alternative.

Computation in the batch layer

Many lambda architecture systems will rely on Hadoop or Spark for the batch layer. Since we don't want to manage a cluster ourselves, we'll have to pick some other serverless system or, at the very least, a managed service. There are a variety of options here.

First, it's possible to implement our MapReduce system entirely using serverless technologies. You'll read about this in Chapter 8, The *MapReduce Pattern*. If you'd rather not build a MapReduce system, there are other services that you can leverage. Both Spark and Hadoop are available within AWS EMR. HDInsight from Azure provides the same or similar functionality to EMR.

Batch processing is a solved problem nowadays, and you should have no problems finding a solution that works for your needs. Since there are so many options for batch processing, you may find it challenging to narrow down your choices.

Processing cryptocurrency prices using lambda architecture

In this chapter, our example application will perform a single task of reading prices in real time for a variety of cryptocurrencies and calculating the average prices by the minute, hour, and day. Of course, this isn't all that useful in the real world because there is so much data on cryptocurrencies already. However, this presents an excellent scenario and dataset for an example application to illustrate this pattern. As is usual in this book, I'll build the application on top of AWS with Python. It's also important to note that none of the concepts are unique to AWS or Python and that this example application is portable to other languages and cloud providers.

You can find the code for this chapter at https://github.com/brianz/ serverless-design-patterns/tree/master/ch7.

System architecture

The architecture of this is perhaps the most complex in this book, even though the implementation itself is relatively simple. As mentioned earlier in this chapter, there are many moving parts in a lambda architecture since it is two distinct systems that work side by side, with each having its own unique set of services. I show a high-level architecture in the following diagram:

This design is somewhat contrived and overly simplified. A system with true scale likely would not be able to get away with a serverless function that calculated historical prices by year, as I do in the batch layer. To fit this example application into a single chapter, I had to make the system relatively simple to demonstrate the pattern and techniques. While this may be an oversimplification of an actual big data system, it does show that the design works on a serverless platform and is even applicable to a decent-sized data problem.

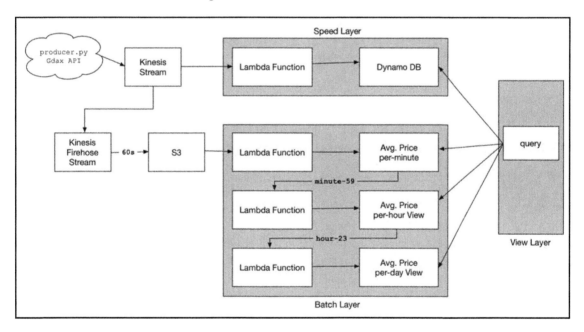

I'll break this down piece by piece and describe how each layer and component works. While there may be a lot going on in this design, each part is quite simple. Most of the complexity of this system comes from the system setup and concepts, instead of application code.

Data producer

To start, we need to have some data to process. In a real system where you are creating the data or wish to send some data *out* from your system, this isn't much of an issue. In our case, we need to pull data in real time from somewhere, and I've chosen the public API from GDAX (`https://www.gdax.com`), which is a digital exchange for cryptocurrencies from Coinbase. This API is suitable for our example application mainly because there are many transactions and there is a WebSocket endpoint that we can subscribe to. A simple script that subscribes to the GDAX WebSocket API and publishes those messages to our Kinesis stream will serve as our data producer.

Speed layer

The speed layer is also relatively simple. Each message published to the Kinesis stream will trigger a Lambda function. This Lambda function will just write the data to DynamoDB so that we can serve data in real time for any queries. With this design, we're set up for a decent amount of real-time load and concurrency. The data producer will deliver data at a reasonably fast rate, perhaps a few messages per second. If there was a burst of traffic and the speed layer started seeing tens or hundreds of messages per second, it would not be a problem.

Since serverless functions and databases such as DynamoDB scale linearly, the speed layer can absorb practically any amount of real-time traffic. There are, of course, provisioning and throughput concerns, as well as maximum concurrent limits to contend. However, these issues are just configuration settings that you can quickly change and increase as needed.

Batch layer

Our batch layer gets a bit more interesting. Some of the details are AWS-centric, but you can carry the general idea across cloud providers. AWS Kinesis Firehose is another version of Kinesis that is designed to transport data in batches to various locations. In this architecture, we'll set up the Kinesis Firehose stream to ingest data from the primary Kinesis stream. I'll also configure the Firehose stream to deliver batches of messages to S3 every minute.

If you have heard about AWS Kinesis but the term Kinesis Firehose is new to you, don't worry. Kinesis Firehose's specialty is loading data into various services, such as S3 and Redshift. A plain Kinesis stream captures data and makes it available for consumption, but that consumption is your responsibility. Kinesis Firehose is useful when you'd like to dump the streaming data to S3 or Redshift automatically.

With a new file being delivered to S3 every minute, we can set up a Lambda function to trigger on that event and perform some work. The work here will be reading the list of messages, calculating the average price per currency, and writing out a new file back to S3. If you follow the flow of time and data, you should be able to see that we can extend this pattern down at different time increments - minutes, hours, days, months, and even years. The general flow and set of triggers look like this:

- Every minute, a Lamba function reads data stored on S3 and calculates the average price for the last minute
- Every hour, a Lamba function reads data stored on S3 and calculates the average price for the last hour
- Every day, a Lamba function reads data stored on S3 and calculates the average price for the previous day

Since data is stored on S3, nothing is stopping this system from evolving to create an entirely new batch layer using more powerful tools such as Spark and Athena.

AWS resources

In my opinion, the most complicated part of this entire system is set up all of the various resources and the interplay between them all. If you count up the number of resources we need to make this system work, the list quickly grows:

- Two S3 buckets
- One Kinesis stream
- One Kinesis Firehose stream
- One DynamoDB table
- Four Lambda functions
- Multiple IAM roles

Not only do we need to create all of the preceding resources, but we need to ensure they can communicate with one another. As is often the case with building with AWS, much of the work involved in managing a stack such as this is getting permissions correct so that the Lambda function can read/write from/to the right S3 buckets, DynamoDB table, or Kinesis stream.

You can see proof of this if we use `cloc` to count the lines of code in this application. Looking at the following output, you'll see that the amount of configuration code in `serverless.yml` is higher than the application code, with 165 lines of YAML configuration to 128 lines of Python code:

```
$ cloc .
        4 text files.
        4 unique files.
        2 files ignored.

github.com/AlDanial/cloc v 1.72 T=0.03 s (96.4 files/s, 12465.5 lines/s)
-------------------------------------------------------------------------
Language            files      blank      comment      code
-------------------------------------------------------------------------
YAML                  1          6           8          157
Python                2         59          22          128
-------------------------------------------------------------------------
SUM:                  3         65          30          285
-------------------------------------------------------------------------
```

I will walk through some interesting bits of the `serverless.yml` file here:

```
service: gdax-lambda-arch

provider:
  name: aws
  runtime: python3.6
  stage: ${env:ENV}
  region: ${env:AWS_REGION}
  iamRoleStatements:
    - Effect: "Allow"
      Action:
        - "s3:GetObject"
        - "s3:ListBucket"
        - "s3:PutObject"
      Resource:
        - "arn:aws:s3:::brianz-gdax-${env:ENV}-firehose"
        - "arn:aws:s3:::brianz-gdax-${env:ENV}-firehose/*"
        - "arn:aws:s3:::brianz-gdax-${env:ENV}-results"
        - "arn:aws:s3:::brianz-gdax-${env:ENV}-results/*"
    - Effect: "Allow"
      Action:
        - "dynamodb:PutItem"
      Resource:
"arn:aws:dynamodb:${self:provider.region}:*:table/brianz-gdax-
${env:ENV}-realtime"
```

First, we need to ensure our Lambda functions will have access to the various resources. In the preceding `iamRoleStatements`, I'm giving various permissions for all Lambda functions in this stack to the two S3 buckets we'll use as well as DynamoDB. This shouldn't come as a big surprise. Our Lambda functions will be reading and writing data from and to S3. Likewise, our speed layer will be writing new records to DynamoDB.

Next, I'll walk through how to create a Kinesis stream that we can write to from our data producer, which, in turn, forwards messages on to a Kinesis Firehose delivery stream. Be warned; this is a bit raw and can seem complicated. I'll break this down bit by bit, hopefully in an order that is comprehensible.

The first step is creating a Kinesis stream. This part is straightforward using the `Resources` section of `serverless.yml`, which is straight-up CloudFormation. In this case, we only need a single shard since our application throughput is reasonably small. If the amount of data you're pushing is larger, you can add additional throughput by increasing the number of shards. The following code snippet is the `resources` section from `serverless.yml` and shows how I'm creating the Kinesis stream:

```
resources:
  Resources:
    # This is the stream which the producer will write to. Any writes
     will trigger a lambda
    # function. The Lambda function will need read access to this
    stream.
    GdaxKinesisStream:
      Type: AWS::Kinesis::Stream
      Properties:
        Name: brianz-gdax-${env:ENV}-kinesis-stream
        RetentionPeriodHours: 24
        ShardCount: 1
```

Next up is the bit which is a bit more complicated. Kinesis Firehose is still a Kinesis stream, that behaves a bit differently as I mentioned earlier. In a standard Kinesis stream, you are responsible for doing something with the messages that producers push onto the stream. Kinesis Firehose, on the other hand, will automatically deliver a batch of messages to some destination. Your choices for final destinations are as follows:

- AWS S3
- AWS Redshift
- AWS Elasticsearch service
- Splunk

We can create a Kinesis Firehose stream by adding some CloudFormation code in the `Resources` block. What we need to create via CloudFormation is the following:

- A Firehose stream that received data from the previous Kinesis stream and batch write data to S3 every 60 seconds
- An IAM role that grants access to Firehose to read/write to/from our S3 buckets and also read the Kinesis stream

This CloudFormation code is a bit verbose. Rather than putting the entire code block here, I'll refer you to the GitHub repository. You can read the full details of setting up the Kinesis Firehose stream at the following URL: `https://github.com/brianz/serverless-design-patterns/blob/master/ch7/serverless/serverless.yml#L47-L113`.

The data source for this Firehose stream is the primary Kinesis stream, which I named `GdaxKinesisStream`. You can see the configuration to use this stream as a data source in the `KinesisStreamSourceConfiguration` and `DeliveryStreamType` keys. These two settings say that we're going to be using a Kinesis stream as a data source, as opposed to putting data directly on this Firehose stream via API calls. It also tells the Firehose stream where to find this source Kinesis stream via the `KinesisStreamSourceConfiguration`, which can be a bit confusing.

Here, `KinesisStreamSourceConfiguration` is comprised of two keys, `KinesisStreamARN` and `RoleARN`. The former, `KinesisStreamARN`, refers to the location of the Kinesis stream we're connecting to. `RoleARN`, on the other hand, has to do with permissions. This referenced role must permit for the reading of the source Kinesis stream. It's a bit too much to cover here, but if you look at the entirety of the configuration, it should make some amount of sense.

Now that we've taken care of the input source, we need to set up the S3 destination configuration in the `S3DestinationConfiguration` key. This configuration is analogous to that of the source stream; we need to give our Firehose stream the data on where to write data with the `BucketARN` and also give it a role with the necessary access.

The other interesting and important part of the `S3DestinationConfiguration` is that it's configured to write data to S3 every 60 seconds or every 5 MB, whichever comes first. Since the GDAX WebSocket feed isn't all that chatty, we can count on hitting the 60-second limit before the buffer in Firehose reaches 5 MB.

From here, we can turn our attention to the Lambda functions that will be running our application code. I've implemented four different Lambda functions, which will handle the following:

- Single events from the Kinesis stream
- S3 objects created every 60 seconds from Kinesis Firehose
- S3 objects created from the aggregated minute views of data
- S3 objects created from the aggregated hour views of data

The configuration of these four Lambda functions is shown as follows:

```
functions:
  ProcessPrice:
    handler: handler.single
    memorySize: 256
    timeout: 3
    events:
      - stream:
          type: kinesis
          arn:
            Fn::GetAtt:
              - GdaxKinesisStream
              - Arn
    environment:
      TABLE_NAME: brianz-gdax-${env:ENV}-realtime
  CalculateMinuteView:
    handler: handler.minute
    memorySize: 256
    timeout: 10
    events:
      - s3:
          bucket: brianz-gdax-${env:ENV}-firehose
          event: s3:ObjectCreated:*
    environment:
      DESTINATION_BUCKET: brianz-gdax-${env:ENV}-results
  CalculateHourlyView:
    handler: handler.hourly
    memorySize: 512
    timeout: 60
    events:
      - s3:
          bucket: brianz-gdax-${env:ENV}-results
          event: s3:ObjectCreated:*
          rules:
            - suffix: '59-minute.json'
  CalculateDailyView:
```

```
handler: handler.daily
memorySize: 1024
timeout: 300
events:
  - s3:
      bucket: brianz-gdax-${env:ENV}-results
      event: s3:ObjectCreated:*
      rules:
        - suffix: '23-hour.json'
```

You can see that the first function, `ProcessPrice`, is triggered upon delivery of a message onto our Kinesis stream. Once this function executes, its job is done. There is no other interaction with this function and any other function.

The next three functions work in coordination. This process starts when `CalculateMinuteView` is triggered when the Firehose stream delivers a new batch of messages every 60 seconds to S3. This function will calculate the average prices using all of the delivered messages and upload a new file to S3 named `MM-minute.json`, where `MM` is a numerical representation of the minute calculated (`00, 01...59`).

Once we reach the end of an hour, this function will write a file named `59-minute.json`. Since that file signifies the end of an hour, we can trigger the `CalculateHourlyView` function to calculate the average prices for the past hour. This function produces files named `HH-hour.json`, where `HH` represents the 24 hours in a day (`00, 01...23`). The same strategy holds true for hours and days. Once a file named `23-hour.json` arrives, it's time to calculate the daily average prices from `CalculateDailyView`.

Data producer

The following example code shows what a simple client application looks like if you're interested in prices for Bitcoin and Ethereum. This code doesn't do anything other than deserializing the JSON payload from each message and printing it to the Terminal:

```
from websocket import WebSocketApp
from json import dumps, loads

URL = "wss://ws-feed.gdax.com"

def on_message(_, message):
    json_message = loads(message)
    print(json_message)
```

```
def on_open(socket):
    products = ["BTC-USD", "ETH-USD"]
    channels = [
        {
            "name": "ticker",
            "product_ids": products,
        },
    ]
    params = {
        "type": "subscribe",
        "channels": channels,
    }
    socket.send(dumps(params))


def main():
    ws = WebSocketApp(URL, on_open=on_open, on_message=on_message)
    ws.run_forever()


if __name__ == '__main__':
    main()
```

Executing this code, I'll see payloads printing out whenever there is a buy or sell transaction for either of the two currencies to which I've subscribed:

```
{'best_ask': '8150',
 'best_bid': '8149.99',
 'high_24h': '8302.73000000',
 'last_size': '0.33846794',
 'low_24h': '8150.00000000',
 'open_24h': '8021.01000000',
 'price': '8150.00000000',
 'product_id': 'BTC-USD',
 'sequence': 5434939366,
 'side': 'buy',
 'time': '2018-03-18T22:48:35.185000Z',
 'trade_id': 39905775,
 'type': 'ticker',
 'volume_24h': '29375.86790154',
 'volume_30d': '633413.03952202'}
```

To get this data into our system, we need a few extra lines of code to publish data into an AWS Kinesis stream. The changes to the preceding client code are quite simple. Upon receiving a new message, I'll check whether the payload is of the correct type, merely by looking for the time key. Some messages that we get back are confirmations to our subscription and do not include the time key, indicating some other message other than a trade. The following code shows these changes and how I use the `boto3` library to publish data to a Kinesis stream:

```
kinesis = boto3.client('kinesis')

def on_message(_, msg):
    json_msg = json.loads(msg)
    if 'time' in json_msg:
        print('Publishing...')
        response = kinesis.put_record(
                StreamName='brianz-gdax-bz-kinesis-stream',
                PartitionKey=json_msg['time'],
                Data=msg + '|||',
        )
        print(response)
    else:
        print(json_msg)
```

This part of our application is completely standalone. I ran this small script on an EC2 instance inside of a `screen` session, so the code continued to run when I logged out. This implementation isn't suitable for a real production system, but it worked just fine for the few days that I ran it. If I were doing this for an actual production system, I'd run this code with some daemon management systems such as `supervisord`, `upstart`, or `runit`.

Speed layer

Our speed layer is the simplest part of the entire system. With the configuration in place—a `single` Lambda function to execute whenever a new stream message arrives—the only work we need to do is decode the data from the message payload, calculate the DynamoDB partition key, and write it to DynamoDB. The following code block shows all of this work in the `single` function, which is processing a single message from AWS Kinesis:

This code is all located in a single `handler.py` function, which goes against a best practice of splitting up application code and decoupling application logic from the cloud-specific bits. However, this application code is for demonstration purposes, and I can get away with breaking some rules for the sake of clarity and brevity. If there were a real system rather than a demo, I would be much more deliberate and organized with this code. Some of the import statements will be used in the batch layer code.

```python
import json
import os
import os.path

from base64 import b64decode
from datetime import datetime

from lambda_arch.aws import (
        get_matching_s3_keys,
        list_s3_bucket,
        read_body_from_s3,
        write_to_dynamo_table,
        write_to_s3,
)

def single(event, context):
    """Process a single message from a kinesis stream and write it to
        DynamoDB"""
    record = event['Records'][0]
    data = record['kinesis']['data']

    # Append on a delimiter since we need to unpack messages which are
    concatenated together when
    # receiving multiple messages from Firehose.
    data = json.loads(b64decode(data).decode().rstrip('|||'))

    # Create our partition key
    data['productTrade'] = '{product_id}|{time}|
    {trade_id}'.format(**data)

    write_to_dynamo_table(os.environ['TABLE_NAME'], data)
```

The result of this code is that every single GDAX transaction we're interested in ends up in our DynamoDB table. The following screenshot shows a subset of the data stored. With the data in DynamoDB, our view layer can quickly look up a set of rows for a particular time range:

productTrade	best_ask	best_bid	high_24h	last_size	low_24h	open_24h	price	product_id
ETH-USD|2018-03-18T23:59:06.682000Z|30825243	538.01	538	587.74000000	4.85780000	538.01000000	551.05000000	538.01000000	ETH-USD
BTC-USD|2018-03-19T00:28:54.655000Z|39918022	8361.78	8361.65	8444.40000000	0.00184000	8361.77000000	7808.91000000	8361.77000000	BTC-USD
BTC-USD|2018-03-19T01:28:04.663000Z|39924120	8127.25	8127.24	8444.40000000	1.18826179	8127.24000000	7795.01000000	8127.24000000	BTC-USD
BTC-USD|2018-03-19T00:42:07.346000Z|39919037	8379.31	8379.3	8444.40000000	0.49288813	8379.31000000	7794.19000000	8379.31000000	BTC-USD
ETH-USD|2018-03-19T03:49:36.515000Z|30638449	526.97	526.96	587.74000000	1.71250000	526.97000000	523.62000000	526.97000000	ETH-USD
BTC-USD|2018-03-19T00:28:06.377000Z|39917906	8340.01	8340	8444.40000000	0.04000000	8340.00000000	7807.08000000	8340.00000000	BTC-USD
BTC-USD|2018-03-19T05:10:28.764000Z|39935922	8204.44	8204.43	8444.40000000	0.02368038	8204.44000000	7588.92000000	8204.44000000	BTC-USD
ETH-USD|2018-03-19T05:01:31.189000Z|30840571	533.01	533	587.74000000	2.16540000	533.01000000	511.40000000	533.01000000	ETH-USD
BTC-USD|2018-03-19T00:36:49.221000Z|39918738	8385.55	8385.54	8444.40000000	0.05660616	8385.54000000	7822.09000000	8385.54000000	BTC-USD
ETH-USD|2018-03-19T01:46:16.917000Z|30833784	524.56	524.55	587.74000000	0.78624812	524.55000000	533.68000000	524.55000000	ETH-USD

Prices for DynamoDB are more dependent on the reads and writes you need for this system. Even though there is no code to trim out data we no longer need (that is, data that is historical and handled the batch layer), it's not a huge concern. Still, if there were a production system, you'd want to consider some techniques on expiring data that is no longer needed.

Batch layer

Whereas our speed layer is only interacting with DynamoDB, our batch layer will just be interacting with S3. There are two distinct types of functions in this layer—the functions that respond to S3 objects that arrive from Firehose, and functions that respond to S3 objects coming from Lambda functions. There isn't all that much difference, but it's important to point out the two different categories.

The following code block, taken from `handler.py`, shows the application code that comprises our batch layer:

```
def _get_bucket_and_key_from_event(event):
    record = event['Records'][0]
    s3 = record['s3']
    bucket = s3['bucket']['name']
    key = s3['object']['key']
    return (bucket, key)

def minute(event, context):
```

```
"""Process an S3 object uploaded to S3 from Kinesis Firehose.

The data format from Firehose is all of the messages from the
`single` function above,
concatenated together. In order to read thse messages, we need to
decode them and split the
string by our own delimiter.

"""
bucket, key = _get_bucket_and_key_from_event(event)
data = read_body_from_s3(bucket, key).decode()

product_prices = {}

lines = [json.loads(l) for l in data.split('|||') if l]
times = []

for line in lines:
    # Only keep track of buys for the average price, since sells
    could be sell orders which are
    # never executed.
    if line.get('side') != 'buy':
        continue

    product_id = line['product_id']
    price = float(line['price'])

    times.append(line['time'])
    if product_id not in product_prices:
        product_prices[product_id] = {'prices': [price]}
    else:
        product_prices[product_id]['prices'].append(price)

if not product_prices:
    return

# Calculate the average for each product
for key in product_prices:
    prices = product_prices[key]['prices']
    product_prices[key]['average'] = sum(prices) * 1.0 /
    len(prices)

# Determine the most recent timestamp from the list of buys so we
can determine the key to
# write.
times.sort()
latest_time = times[-1]
latest_dt = datetime.strptime(latest_time, DT_FORMAT)
```

```
        destination_bucket = os.environ['DESTINATION_BUCKET']
        new_key = latest_dt.strftime('%Y/%m/%d/%H/%M-minute.json')
        new_payload = json.dumps(product_prices, indent=2)

        print('Uploading to', destination_bucket, new_key)

        write_to_s3(destination_bucket, new_key, new_payload)


    def _aggregate_prices(event, period='hour'):
        """Aggregate average prices for a particular time slice"""
        bucket, key = _get_bucket_and_key_from_event(event)
        key_root = os.path.dirname(key)

        product_prices = {}

        for key in get_matching_s3_keys(bucket, prefix=key_root + '/',
        suffix='-minute.json'):
            data = read_body_from_s3(bucket, key).decode()
            minute_prices = json.loads(data)

            for product_id, payload in minute_prices.items():
                prices = payload['prices']
                if product_id not in product_prices:
                    product_prices[product_id] = {'prices': prices}
                else:
                    product_prices[product_id]['prices'].extend(prices)

        for key in product_prices:
            prices = product_prices[key]['prices']
            average_price = sum(prices) * 1.0 / len(prices)
            product_prices[key]['average'] = average_price

        new_key = '%s-%s.json' % (key_root, period)
        new_payload = json.dumps(product_prices, indent=2)

        print('Uploading to', bucket, new_key)

        write_to_s3(bucket, new_key, new_payload)


    def hourly(event, context):
        _aggregate_prices(event, period='hour')


    def daily(event, context):
        _aggregate_prices(event, period='day')
```

Batch processing starts with the `minute` function. Again, this function starts when a new file arrives in S3 from our Firehose stream. At this point, we can be assured that the `minute` function is invoked once a minute based on our configuration. We don't need to go through this line by line, but we can look at the final results as well as some small tricks.

You may notice the line that splits data using `split('||||')`. Firehose will concatenate records together before delivering to any data source. The AWS documentation on Kinesis Firehose explicitly states this, but it's still easy to overlook:

> *"For data delivery to Amazon S3, Kinesis Firehose concatenates multiple incoming records based on buffering configuration of your delivery stream and then delivers them to Amazon S3 as an S3 object. You may want to add a record separator at the end of each record before you send it to Kinesis Firehose so that you can divide a delivered S3 object to individual records."*

The preceding has been quoted from `https://docs.aws.amazon.com/firehose/latest/dev/basic-deliver.html`.

If you look back up at the data producer, you can see that we're appending the `'||||'` string to each message. With this delimiter, it's possible for us to break apart individual messages in this function.

The final results that the `minute` function uploads to S3 have the following form. For each currency, it includes the list of individual buy prices along with the average price:

```
{
  "BTC-USD": {
    "prices": [
      8173.59,
      8173.59,
      8173.59,
      8173.59,
      8173.59,
      8173.59,
      8173.59,
      8173.59,
      8174.99,
      8176.17,
      8176.17
    ],
    "average": 8174.186363636362
  },
  "ETH-USD": {
    "prices": [
      533.01,
```

```
        533.01,
        533.01,
        533.01,
        533.01,
        533.01
    ],
    "average": 533.0100000000001
  }
}
```

Our `CalculateHourlyView` executes once a file named `59-minute.json` arrives in S3. The arrival of this S3 object signifies the end of an hour, so it's time to calculate the average prices for the entire hour. That work for the hour calculation, as well as the calculation of the daily average, is all wrapped up in the `_aggregate_prices` function. By using the prefix of the S3 object that triggers the functions, we'll only scan through a subset of the S3 records that are used in the calculation of the averages. For example, when a new S3 object arrives with a key name of `$BUCKET/2018/03/19/04/59-minute.json`, our application code can pick apart the `$BUCKET/2018/03/19/04` prefix and only scan files in that location. When an S3 object arrives named `$BUCKET/2018/03/19/23-hour.json`, the daily function will scan through files with the `$BUCKET/2018/03/19` prefix.

Results

After running this system for a few days, I was able to produce many S3 files as expected, as well as keeping track of each trade in DynamoDB. As I mentioned earlier in this chapter, implementing some view layer wasn't feasible for this example system. However, querying DynamoDB is quite easy, provided primary keys and sort keys are set up correctly. Any view layer that needed to get historical data could easily grab files from S3.

The following screenshot shows listings of S3 files for a given hour. Each file has the format shown earlier with individual prices, along with the pre-computed average for each currency:

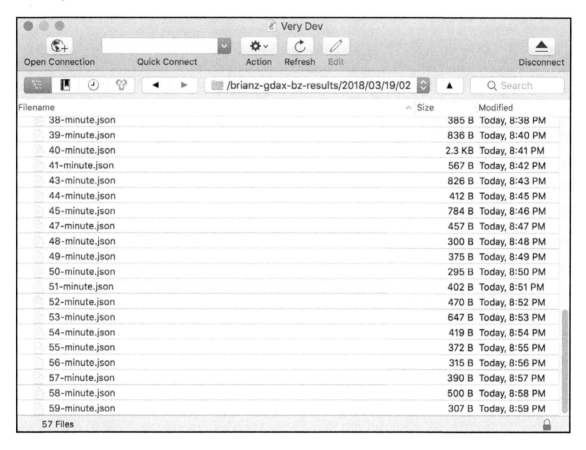

Looking one level up in the S3 hierarchy, we can see the hour files that contain the average prices:

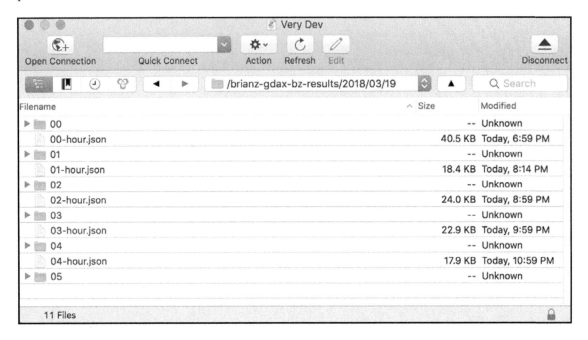

Summary

In this chapter, we discussed the Lambda pattern at a conceptual level as well as in detail. I walked through an example implementation with serverless technologies to calculate average cryptocurrency prices for different time slices. Our example application was fed by a simple script that receives data from the GDAX WebSocket API. This data producer script published data to a single AWS Kinesis stream, which, in turn, triggered a series of events, ultimately resulting in real-time updates to DynamoDB and triggering batch jobs to calculate historical views of the minute, hourly, and daily average prices for multiple cryptocurrencies.

I discussed when the Lambda pattern may be appropriate and the types of data for which it's well suited. We talked through various systems and services that one may leverage when building a lambda architecture using serverless technologies. I introduced AWS Kinesis and AWS Kinesis Firehose, which are streaming systems you may leverage for real-time applications.

While the details of a Lambda pattern implementation can be quite intricate, readers should have a decent understanding of its advantages, disadvantages, and when they should consider it.

In the next chapter, I'll cover the MapReduce pattern and work through an example where we will build our very own serverless implementation of this pattern.

8
The MapReduce Pattern

MapReduce is a common data processing pattern made famous by Google and now implemented in various systems and frameworks, most notably Apache Hadoop. Nowadays, this pattern is familiar and easy to understand at its core, but running large-scale systems such as Hadoop comes with its own set of challenges and cost of ownership. In this chapter, we'll show how this pattern can be implemented on your own using serverless technologies.

Implementing big data applications in a serverless environment may seem counter-intuitive due to the computing limitations of FaaS. Certain types of problems fit very well into a serverless ecosystem, especially considering we practically have unlimited file storage with distributed filesystems such as AWS S3. Additionally, MapReduce's magic is not so much in the application of an algorithm, but in the distribution of computing power such that computation is performed in parallel.

In this chapter, we will discuss the application and development of a MapReduce pattern in a serverless environment. I'll cover the use cases for such a design and when it may or may not be a good fit. I'll also show how simple this pattern is within a serverless platform and what you should take into consideration before embarking on building your system.

At the end of this chapter, you can expect to understand the following topics:

- What problem MapReduce solves and when it may be appropriate to implement in a serverless environment
- Design and scaling considerations when applying this pattern on your own
- How to implement your own MapReduce serverless system to count occurrences of from-to combinations from a corpus of email messages
- How to use the Fanout pattern as a sub-component of the MapReduce pattern

Introduction to MapReduce

MapReduce as a pattern and programming model has been around for many years, arising from parallel computing research and industry implementations. Most famously, MapReduce hit the mainstream with Google's 2004 paper entitled *MapReduce—Simplified Data Processing on Large Clusters* (`https://research.google.com/archive/mapreduce.html`). Much of the benefit of Google's initial MapReduce implementation was:

- Automatic parallelization and distribution
- Fault-tolerance
- I/O scheduling
- Status and monitoring

If you take a step back and look at that list, it should look familiar. FaaS systems such as AWS Lambda give us most of these benefits. While status and monitoring aren't inherently baked into FaaS platforms, there are ways to ensure our functions are executing successfully. On that same topic, MapReduce systems were initially, and still are, very often, managed at the OS level, meaning operators are in charge of taking care of crashed or otherwise unhealthy nodes.

The preceding list of benefits is listed in the following slide from a presentation-like form of the research paper: `https://research.google.com/archive/mapreduce-osdi04-slides/index-auto-0002.html`

Not too long after Google's 2004 MapReduce paper, the Apache Hadoop project was born. Hadoop's goal was an open source implementation of the MapReduce pattern for big data processing. Since then, Hadoop has arguably become the most popular MapReduce framework today. Additionally, the term *Hadoop* has evolved to include many other frameworks for big data processing and refers more to the ecosystem of tools rather than the single framework.

As powerful and popular as Hadoop is, it's a complicated beast in practice. In order to run a Hadoop cluster of any significance, one needs to run and master Zookeeper and **HDFS (Hadoop Distributed File System)**, in addition to the Hadoop master and worker nodes themselves. For those unfamiliar with these tools and all of the DevOps ownership that comes with them, running a Hadoop cluster is not only daunting but impractical.

MapReduce example

If you've never worked with a MapReduce framework or system, the overall concepts are not incredibly complex. In fact, we can implement a single-process and single-threaded MapReduce system in a few lines of code.

Overall, MapReduce is designed to extract a specific bit of information from a body of data and distill it down into some final result. That may sound very vague and arbitrary, and it is. The beauty of MapReduce is that one can apply it to so many different problems. A few examples should better demonstrate what MapReduce is and how you can use it.

A *Hello World* MapReduce program counts the number of occurrences of a particular word in a body of text. The following code block does this with a few lines of Python code:

```
lorem = """
Lorem ipsum dolor sit amet, consectetur adipiscing elit. Etiam ac
pulvinar mi. Proin nec mollis
tellus. In neque risus, rhoncus nec tellus eu, laoreet faucibus eros.
Ut malesuada dui vel ipsum
...
venenatis ullamcorper ex sed eleifend. Nam nec pharetra elit.
"""

words = (w.strip() for w in lorem.split())

def mapper(word):
    return (word, 1)

def reducer(mapper_results):
    results = {}
    for (word, count) in mapper_results:
        if word in results:
            results[word] += count
        else:
            results[word] = count
    return results

mapper_results = map(mapper, words)
reducer_results = reducer(mapper_results)
print(reducer_results)
```

First, this code performs a mapping phase that emits a two element tuple for every occurrence of a work. For example, a given word would emit ('amet', 1) for the word amet. The result from this mapping phase is a list of (word, 1) pairs, where the 1 simply means we've encountered the word.

The job of the reducer is to aggregate the mapper's output into some final format. In our case, we'd like a final tally of the number of occurrences for each word. Reading through the preceding `reducer` function, it should be obvious how I'm doing that. A snippet from the final output is shown in the following code block. You can see that `amet` only shows up once in the `Lorem`, `ipsum` text blog, but `sit` shows up nine times:

```
{
    'Lorem': 1,
    'ipsum': 4,
    'dolor': 3,
    'sit': 9,
    'amet,': 1,
    ...
}
```

Role of the mapper

The primary purpose of the `mapper` is to emit data that the reducer will later aggregate into a final. In this trivial example, each occurrence of a word results in a (`word`, `1`) pair since we're giving a single appearance of a word a score of `1`. We very well could have emitted the word by itself (that is, `'amet'`) and put the score of `1` in the reducer; however, this would have made the code less general. If we wanted to give a heavier weighting to certain words, we'd merely change our mapper to output a different number based on the word and would leave our `reducer` code as-is.

The following code block shows how we would give the word `amet` a score of `10` while all other words count as `1`. Of course, this is no longer counting word occurrences but instead scoring words:

```
def mapper(word):
    if word == 'amet':
        return (word, 10)
    else:
        return (word, 1)
```

If we were computing something completely different, you should see now that we'd need to update the mapper function. Some examples of additional calculations we could make based on this Lorem ipsum text could be:

- Number of uppercase letters in a word
- Number of vowels in a word
- The average length of a word

Some of these would require changes to the reducer step, which we'll cover in the following section.

Role of the reducer

While the mapper's job is to extract and emit some form of data to be aggregated, the reducer's job is to perform that aggregation. In this example, the reducer receives the full list of (word, 1) pairs and just adds up the counts (1, in this case) for each word. If we were to perform a different aggregation, the reducer function would need to change.

Rather than counting the number of occurrences, let's calculate the average length of a word. In this case, both our mapper and our reducer will need updating with the more significant changes happening within the reducer. The following code block changes our example to calculate the average word length for a body of text broken up into words:

```
def mapper(word):
    return len(word)

def reducer(mapper_results):
    results = list(mapper_results)
    total_words = len(results)
    total_len = sum(results)
    return total_len / total_words
```

As in the prior example, the mapper is quite dumb and only returns the word length. Since this example doesn't rely on anything specific to the words, there is no need to return the word itself. The reducer code becomes even more straightforward. The input to the reducer is now a list of numbers. To calculate the average, it's a simple task of returning the total divided by the number of elements.

MapReduce architecture

The real magic behind MapReduce implementations such as Hadoop is the distribution and parallelization of computation. Our trivial example would work well running on your laptop even when the input data was several megabytes. However, imagine a case where you would like to perform some analysis like this on data that is hundreds of gigabytes, terabytes, or even in the petabyte range.

Real MapReduce systems use two essential tricks to do this work efficiently. One is working in parallel as I've already mentioned. This means, for example, that multiple instances that do the computation comprise a Hadoop system or cluster. The other trick is co-locating data with the worker node that does the work. Data co-location reduces network traffic and speeds up overall processing.

Mappers begin their work on a subset of the input data. You can imagine that when working on petabytes of data, there could be hundreds or thousands of nodes involved. Once the mappers have completed their job, they send their data to the reducers for final processing. The following diagram shows the details of this architecture from a conceptual standpoint:

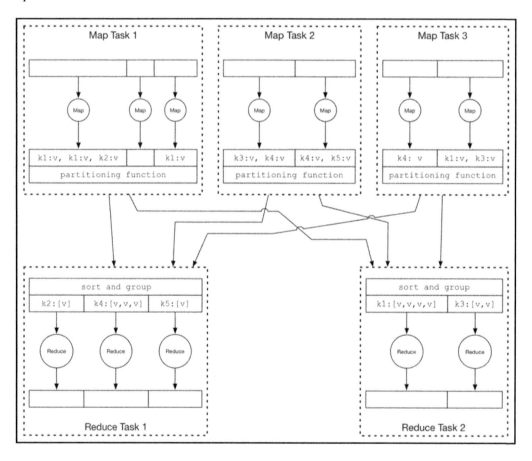

Image adapted from *MapReduce:
Simplified Data Processing on Large Clusters*, Jeff Dean, Sanjay Ghemawat
Google, Inc. https://research.google.com/archive/mapreduce-osdi04-slides/index-auto-0008.html

A key phase in Hadoop is the *shuffle* phase, labeled **partitioning function** in the previous diagram. The arrows coming out of the Map Tasks show that a subset of mapper data will be sent to various reducers. In Hadoop, all output for specific keys is sent to the same reducer node. For example, in our case of the word count, the key (`'amet'`, `1`) would be sent to the same reducer machine/node regardless of which mapper emitted that key. The reason behind this is to reduce network latency and reduce complexity for the reducers. By guaranteeing that a reducer has all of the data needed to perform its final reduce task, reducers are both faster and simpler to implement. Without this guarantee, the framework would need to designate a master reducer and crawl horizontally to final all the necessary data. Not only is that complex, but it's also slow because of all of the network latency.

There are many details that we cannot cover in a system as complex as Hadoop. If you have unanswered questions at this point, I'd encourage you to do some more investigation on your own. Hopefully, this discussion has been enough to set the stage for our serverless implementation of MapReduce in the next section.

MapReduce serverless architecture

MapReduce on a serverless platform is very different than in a system such as Hadoop. Most of the differences occur on the operational and system architecture side of things. Another huge difference is the limited processing power and memory we have with our FaaS. Because FaaS providers put in hard limits for both temporary storage space and memory, there are some problems that you cannot realistically solve with a serverless MapReduce implementation.

The good news is that the foundational ideas in the MapReduce design still hold true. If you look back up at the start of the initial list of benefits provided by MapReduce, we naturally get many of these for free, albeit with a few caveats. MapReduce truly shines, due in large part to the parallelization of computation. We have that with serverless functions. Similarly, much work goes into ensuring Hadoop nodes are healthy and able to perform work. Again, we get that for free with serverless functions.

A significant feature we do *not* get is the co-location of our data and the processing of that data. Our distributed filesystem in this example will be AWS S3. The only way to get data to our serverless functions is to either send that data via API or have our functions fetch the data across the network. Hadoop storage and computing co-location mean that each mapper node processes the data that it has stored locally, using the HDFS. This drastically cuts down on the amount of data being transferred over the network and is an implementation detail that makes the entire system possible.

Before you start your implementation of this pattern, ask yourself whether you can segment your data to a point where processing it with a Lambda function is possible. If your input data is 100 GB, it's feasible that you may have 100 functions handling 1 GB each, even with paying the penalty of network bandwidth. However, it won't be practical to expect a reducer to produce a 100 GB output file since it would need to hold that in memory to calculate the final result.

Either way, we need to consider the size of the data we're processing, both concerning reads and writes. Fortunately, it's easy to scale out Lambda functions, so executing 10s or 100s of Lambda functions are of little difference.

I've drawn the overall architecture of our system in the following block diagram. We'll walk through each of the five steps in detail. For this diagram, the actual problem at hand is less important than the real architecture:

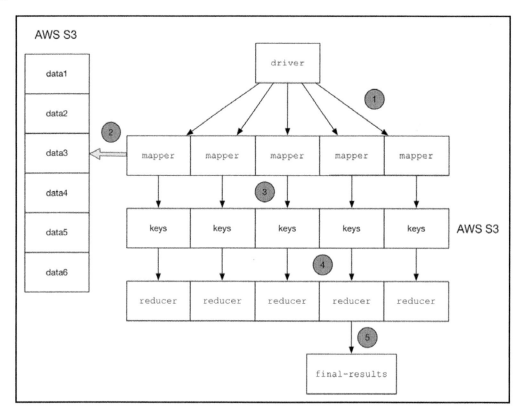

Our implementation can be broken down into five significant steps:

1. We trigger a `driver` function that lists the content of a particular bucket on S3. For each file in S3, the driver triggers an SNS event that ultimately triggers a `mapper` function. Each `mapper` function receives a different payload that corresponds to a file in S3.

2. Mappers read data from S3 and perform a first level aggregation.

3. The mappers write the intermediate *keys* result to S3.

4. The data writes to S3 trigger reducers. Every time a reducer is triggered, it checks whether all of the intermediate *keys* data is ready. If not, the reducer does nothing.

5. Once all of the *keys* data is ready, a reducer will run a final aggregation across all intermediate *keys* files and write the final results to S3.

Many things are going on here, each of which we will discuss in detail.

Processing Enron emails with serverless MapReduce

I've based our example application on the Enron email corpus, which is publicly available on Kaggle. This data is made up of some 500,000 emails from the Enron corporation. In total, this dataset is approximately 1.5 GB. What we will be doing is counting the number of From-To emails. That is, for each person who *sent* an email, we will generate a count of the number of times they sent *to* a particular person.

Anyone may download and work with this dataset: `https://www.kaggle.com/wcukierski/enron-email-dataset`. The original data from Kaggle comes as a single file in CSV format. To make this data work with this example MapReduce program, I broke the single ~1.4 GB file into roughly 100 MB chunks. During this example, it's important to remember that we are starting from 14 separate files on S3.

The data format in our dataset is a CSV with two columns, the first being the email message location (on the mail server, presumably) and the second being the full email message. Since we're only concerned with the `From` and `To` fields, we'll just concern ourselves with the email message.

The code for this chapter may be found at: `https://github.com/brianz/serverless-design-patterns/tree/master/ch8`

Driver function

To initiate the entire process, some event needs to be triggered. Here, we'll do this manually. The `driver` function is responsible for setting up the whole job and invoking the mappers in parallel. We'll accomplish this using some straightforward techniques.

By their nature, MapReduce jobs are batch-oriented, meaning they start up, do their work, write the results somewhere, and finally shut down. As such, doing this on some schedule (whether it be hourly, nightly, or weekly) makes sense. If we were doing this for real where the input data was changing, it would be trivial to set up this `driver` function to run on a schedule.

As usual, the entry point for all our functions is the `handler.py` file, which I have not shown. The `driver` function will invoke the `crawl` function located in `mapreduce/driver.py`. The crawl function contains all of the logic, so we'll focus on this. I've shown the full listing of `mapreduce/driver.py` in the following code block:

```python
import time
import uuid

from .aws import (
        list_s3_bucket,
        publish_to_sns,
)


def crawl(bucket_name, prefix=''):
    """Entrypoint for a map-reduce job.

    The function is responsible for crawling a particular S3 bucket and
    publishing map jobs
    asyncrhonously using SNS where the mapping is 1-to-1, file-to-sns.

    It's presumed that lambda mapper functions are hooked up to the SNS
    topic. These Lambda
    mappers will each work on a particular file.
```

```
"""
print('Starting at: %s: %s' % (time.time(), time.asctime(), ))

# Unique identifer for the entire map-reduce run
run_id = str(uuid.uuid4())
mapper_data = [
        {
            'bucket': bucket,
            'job_id': str(uuid.uuid4()),
            'key': key,
            'run_id': run_id,
        } for (bucket, key) in list_s3_bucket(bucket_name, prefix)
]

# Let's add in the total number of jobs which will be kicked off.
num_mappers = len(mapper_data)

for i, mapper_dict in enumerate(mapper_data):
    mapper_dict['total_jobs'] = num_mappers
    mapper_dict['job_id'] = i
    publish_to_sns(mapper_dict)
```

One implementation detail we will use is uniquely identifying each MapReduce run using a UUID. In this way, it will be easy for a given run to find the necessary files to work within S3. Without this, it would be much harder or impossible to know what files a given Lambda function should be looking at or processing.

As this crawler process starts, it lists the content of our input bucket on S3. Each file or S3 key the crawler finds is wrapped up into a payload that it later uses to trigger the mappers. In the preceding code block, you can see the format of the payload objects. Downstream, the reducers will need to know how many total mappers were executed so that they know when to begin their work. The final for loop will amend each payload with the total number of mapper jobs being executed along with a unique job_id, which is merely an integer from 0 to number_of_mappers - 1.

To trigger the mappers in parallel, the crawler sends an SNS event. We could have accomplished this with mostly the same result by invoking the mappers directly. Personally, I prefer using SNS in these cases since the behavior is asynchronous by default. If you remember back to the chapter on the Fanout pattern, invoking an asynchronously Lambda function requires you to pass the correct argument to the Lambda invoke API. In this case, there isn't anything special to remember, and our code can trigger the event in the most basic fashion. In this particular case, there is otherwise little difference between the two methods and either would work.

What is important to recognize here is that an SNS event is triggered for each file the crawl function finds in S3. In our example, there are 14 different files of approximately 100 MB each. Fourteen records mean that we will have 14 mapper functions running in parallel, each processing a specific S3 file. Mappers know which file to process because we've told them via the `bucket` and `key` arguments in the payload.

Astute readers may recognize this sub-pattern in the `crawl` function. A single function spawning multiple processes asynchronously is exactly what we discussed and implemented in the earlier chapters concerning the Fanout pattern. As noted in that chapter, you may use Fanout inside other more complex patterns such as MapReduce. As you move along with your serverless systems, look for opportunities to reuse patterns as they make sense when composing larger and more complex systems.

Mapper implementation

Now that we have a way to invoke mappers in parallel, let's look at the logic that they implement. Remember again that our task is to count the number of (From, To) email addresses from a large number of email messages.

The work involved here is relatively straightforward. With each mapper receiving a unique 100 MB file, each invocation will perform the same set of tasks:

1. Download the file from S3
2. Parse each message and extract the From and To fields, making sure to account for group sends (where the From user sends to multiple To addresses)
3. Count the number of (From, To) occurrences
4. Write the results to S3

I've shown the full listing of `mapreduce/mapper.py` in the following code block:

```python
import csv
import itertools
import json
import os
import sys
import time

import email.parser

# Make sure we can read big csv files
csv.field_size_limit(sys.maxsize)
```

```
from .aws import (
        download_from_s3,
        write_csv_to_s3,
)


def _csv_lines_from_filepath(filepath, delete=True):
    with open(filepath, 'rt') as fh:
        reader = csv.DictReader(fh, fieldnames=('file', 'message'))
        for row in reader:
            yield row

    if delete:
        os.remove(filepath)


def map(event):
    message = json.loads(event['Records'][0]['Sns']['Message'])

    total_jobs = message['total_jobs']
    run_id = message['run_id']
    job_id = message['job_id']

    counts = {}

    bucket = os.environ['REDUCE_RESULTS_BUCKET']

    tmp_file = download_from_s3(message['bucket'], message['key'])

    parser = email.parser.Parser()

    for line in _csv_lines_from_filepath(tmp_file):
        msg = line['message']
        eml = parser.parsestr(msg, headersonly=True)
        _from = eml['From']

        _tos = eml.get('To')
        if not _tos:
            continue

        _tos = (t.strip() for t in _tos.split(','))

        for from_to in itertools.product([_from], _tos):
            if from_to not in counts:
                counts[from_to] = 1
            else:
                counts[from_to] += 1
```

```
if not counts:
    return

metadata = {
        'job_id': str(job_id),
        'run_id': str(run_id),
        'total_jobs': str(total_jobs),
}

key = 'run-%s/mapper-%s-done.csv' % (run_id, job_id)
write_csv_to_s3(bucket, key, counts, Metadata=metadata)
```

As with the crawler, there isn't much complexity to this mapper code. To count the number of (From, To) combinations I'm using a basic Python dictionary with the keys being a two-element tuple of (From, To) and the value being a number. The other bits of code around this deal with downloading the file from S3, parsing the email message, and calculating all of the (From, To) combinations, when an email contains multiple To recipients.

Once the final result is ready, the mapper writes a new CSV file to S3. Using the Metadata argument, we can communicate any extra information to our reducers without having to write to the file content. Here, we need to tell the reducers a few extra things such as:

- The run_id, which is used to limit the files scanned and processed since we're sharing an S3 bucket across MapReduce runs
- The job_id, so we know which individual mapper job has finished
- The total number of jobs, so the reducer will only start once all mappers have completed

Reducer implementation

At this point in our MapReduce run, the mappers have run and eventually write their intermediate output data to S3. Mappers were triggered by an invocation of SNS events on a given SNS topic. We will set up the reducers to be triggered based on an s3:ObjectCreated event. Taking a look at the serverless.yml file, we can see how I've done this:

```
functions:
  Reducer:
    handler: handler.reducer
    events:
      - s3:
          bucket: brianz-${env:ENV}-mapreduce-results
```

```
event: s3:ObjectCreated:*
rules:
   - suffix: '-done.csv'
```

The s3 section in the events block says: *Whenever a new object is uploaded to s3 with the –*
done.csv suffix, invoke the hander.reducer *function.*

Just as the mapper was reasonably straightforward, so too is the reducer. Much of the logic
in the reducer is a matter of coordination, determining whether it's time to do its work. Let's
enumerate the steps in the reducer to show precisely what it's doing:

1. Extra metadata from the S3 file that triggered the invocation. Key pieces of data
   in that Metadata attribute are necessary for coordination of the entire process.
2. List the contents of our S3 bucket and run_id prefix to determine whether all
   mappers have finished.
3. If there are still reducers running, there is nothing more to do. If all of the
   reducers *have* finished, start the final reduce step.
4. Write an empty file to S3, as a way to claim a lock on the final reduce step.
   Without this, it would be possible for two or more reducers to run concurrently if
   they were invoked at nearly the same time.
5. In the final reduce step, download all of the intermediate files from the mappers
   and perform the final aggregation.
6. Write the final output to S3.

The full listing of mapreduce/reducer.py is shown as follows:

```
import csv
import json
import time
import os
import uuid
import io

from .aws import (
        download_from_s3,
        list_s3_bucket,
        read_from_s3,
        s3_file_exists,
        write_to_s3,
        write_csv_to_s3,
)


def _get_final_results_key(run_id):
```

```python
        return 'run-%s/FinalResults.csv' % (run_id, )


    def _get_batch_job_prefix(run_id):
        return 'run-%s/mapper-' % (run_id, )


    def _get_job_metadata(event):
        s3_record = event['Records'][0]['s3']
        bucket = s3_record['bucket']['name']
        key = s3_record['object']['key']

        s3_obj = read_from_s3(bucket, key)
        job_metadata = s3_obj['Metadata']

        run_id = job_metadata['run_id']
        total_jobs = int(job_metadata['total_jobs'])
        return (bucket, run_id, total_jobs)


    def reduce(event):
        bucket, run_id, total_jobs = _get_job_metadata(event)

        # count up all of the final done files and make sure they equal the
        total number of mapper jobs
        prefix = _get_batch_job_prefix(run_id)
        final_files = [
                (bucket, key) for (_, key) in \
                list_s3_bucket(bucket, prefix) \
                if key.endswith('-done.csv')
        ]
        if len(final_files) != total_jobs:
            print(
                'Reducers are still running...skipping. Expected %d done
                 files but found %s' % (
                    total_jobs, len(final_files),
                )
            )
            return

        # Let's put a lock file here so we can claim that we're finishing
        up the final reduce step
        final_results_key = _get_final_results_key(run_id)
        if s3_file_exists(bucket, final_results_key):
            print('Skipping final reduce step')
            return

        # write blank file to lock the final reduce step
```

```
        write_to_s3(bucket, final_results_key, {})

        print('Starting final reduce phase')

        s3_mapper_files = list_s3_bucket(bucket, prefix)

        final_results = {}

        for (bucket, key) in s3_mapper_files:
            print('reading', key)

            tmp_fn = download_from_s3(bucket, key)

            with open(tmp_fn, 'r') as csv_fh:
                reader = csv.DictReader(csv_fh, fieldnames=('key',
                'count'))
                for line in reader:
                    key = line['key']
                    count = int(line['count'])

                    if key in final_results:
                        final_results[key] += count
                    else:
                        final_results[key] = count

        print('Final final_results:', len(final_results))
        print('Writing fiinal output data')
        write_csv_to_s3(bucket, final_results_key, final_results)
```

Stepping through this code is hopefully a simple exercise. As you can see, most of the work is that of coordination, reading data from S3, and determining whether it's time to perform the final reduce step. You can see that when the last mapper is finished, the total number of intermediate files will equal the number of mapper jobs initially invoked.

Looking at S3, we can see the final results after a successful run:

Filename	Size	Modified
▼ 📁 run-37079b8e-a5c4-4781-b024-61aab8d8c374	--	Unknown
FinalResults.csv	18.2 MB	Today, 1:25 PM
mapper-0-done.csv	2.7 MB	Today, 1:24 PM
mapper-1-done.csv	2.6 MB	Today, 1:24 PM
mapper-2-done.csv	2.1 MB	Today, 1:24 PM
mapper-3-done.csv	2.4 MB	Today, 1:25 PM
mapper-4-done.csv	2.4 MB	Today, 1:24 PM
mapper-5-done.csv	1.9 MB	Today, 1:25 PM
mapper-6-done.csv	1.1 MB	Today, 1:24 PM
mapper-7-done.csv	2.7 MB	Today, 1:24 PM
mapper-8-done.csv	1.7 MB	Today, 1:24 PM
mapper-9-done.csv	2.9 MB	Today, 1:24 PM
mapper-10-done.csv	3.3 MB	Today, 1:24 PM
mapper-11-done.csv	2.5 MB	Today, 1:24 PM
mapper-12-done.csv	2.2 MB	Today, 1:24 PM
mapper-13-done.csv	2.1 MB	Today, 1:24 PM
▶ 📁 run-87424cde-8c83-4744-aeb5-2cb215998735	--	Unknown

Here, each mapper job created a unique `mapper-job_id-done.csv` file. Once all 14 files arrived in S3, the final reducer step began, which ultimately read all 14 files and produced the `FinalResults.csv` file. You can also see how individual MapReduce runs are segregated in S3 with the UUID embedded in each S3 key path. This is necessary so that each run can operate independently and know which files it should be scanning through in S3. Again, a critical check in the final reducer step is to determine whether all of the mappers have finished their work and uploaded their results to S3. The reducer will determine the mapper's state of completeness by counting the number of files in S3 using the `run_id` as a prefix during the S3 scan. If the number of these `-done.csv` files is less than the total number of mappers, they have not all completed.

If we take a look at `FinalResults.csv`, we can see the count of the following:

```
$ head FinalResults.csv
"('phillip.allen@enron.com', 'tim.belden@enron.com')",31
"('phillip.allen@enron.com', 'john.lavorato@enron.com')",63
"('phillip.allen@enron.com', 'leah.arsdall@enron.com')",3
"('phillip.allen@enron.com', 'randall.gay@enron.com')",23
"('phillip.allen@enron.com', 'greg.piper@enron.com')",6
"('phillip.allen@enron.com', 'david.l.johnson@enron.com')",4
"('phillip.allen@enron.com', 'john.shafer@enron.com')",4
"('phillip.allen@enron.com', 'joyce.teixeira@enron.com')",3
```

```
"('phillip.allen@enron.com', 'mark.scott@enron.com')",3
"('phillip.allen@enron.com', 'zimam@enron.com')",4
```

What is neat about this is that the processing of all 1.5 GB of data happens quite quickly. In my testing, the system produced the final results after approximately 50 seconds.

Understanding the limitations of serverless MapReduce

MapReduce on a serverless platform can work very well. However, there are limitations that you need to keep in mind. First and foremost, memory, storage, and time limits will ultimately determine whether this pattern is possible for your dataset. Additionally, systems such as Hadoop are frameworks that one may use for any analysis. When implementing MapReduce in a serverless context, you will likely be implementing a system that will solve a particular problem.

I find that a serverless MapReduce implementation is viable when your final dataset is relatively small (a few hundred megabytes) such that your reducer can process all of the data without going over the memory limits for your FaaS provider. I will talk through some of the details behind that sentiment in the following.

Memory limits

In the reducer phase, all of the data produced from the mappers must, at some point, be read and stored in memory. In our example application, the reducer reads 14 separate files sequentially and builds up a mapping of (From, To) addresses with corresponding numbers. The number of unique combinations for this dataset is 311,209. That is, our final results file is a CSV with just over 311,000 lines for a total of 18.2 MB. As you can imagine, this is well within the boundaries of a single Lambda function; reading 14 files keeping approximately 18 MB of data in memory isn't beyond the abilities of an individual Lambda function.

Imagine a case where we are counting IP addresses from a large number of large log files along with some other metric. IP addresses have the form `192.168.1.200` and can vary in their lengths when represented as a string. For this example, presume the format of the lines produced by the reducer will look like `176.100.206.13,0.6088772`, which is a single line of CSV with the IP address in the first column and a made-up metric in the second column. This string is 24 bytes long. Currently, the maximum memory for a single Lambda function is 3 GB, which is 3,221,225,472 bytes. With an average length of 24 bytes per IP address, we can hold less than 135 million unique IP addresses in memory—`3,221,225,472 / 24 = 134,217,728`. There are approximately 3,706,452,992 unique IP4 addresses. It's clear that a serverless MapReduce implementation for working with IP addresses would break down if the number of unique IP addresses in the dataset was in the order of 100 million or more.

Storage limits

FaaS systems have storage limits just like they have memory limits. If you have looked at the code I've implemented in the example application, you may have noticed that I download files and store them in `/tmp` before processing them. This strategy isn't necessary, as it's possible to read data from S3 and store it in memory. In my testing, I found performance gains when downloading the files to disk and then reading them with the standard filesystem `open` calls. Some of the CSV APIs I was using were also easier to use with a real file handler rather than a String in memory.

When downloading data and storing the files locally, you must keep in mind the storage limits enforced by your FaaS provider. For example, AWS Lambda currently gives you 512 MB of ephemeral storage in `/tmp`. If you have a need to download files larger than 512 MB, you would need to find another solution, such as reading data directly into memory and skipping disks entirely. Reading large data into memory will cut into your memory for the final result set, so the balance of getting this right when dealing with huge datasets can be tricky.

Time limits

The final limit to keep in mind is the execution limit. Even if your MapReduce implementation can stay within the storage and memory limits of your FaaS provider, you will still have to ensure your functions complete their work within a given time limit. As of this writing, AWS Lambda functions have an upper limit of 300 seconds. If any part of your MapReduce system takes longer than 300 seconds, you're out of luck and will have to find a workaround. With mappers, it's relatively simple to break the work into smaller pieces and execute more concurrent mappers. However, when the reducer runs, it must load all of the mapper data to compile it down to the final result set. If this takes longer than 300 seconds, it will be impossible to produce the final results.

Exploring alternate implementations

While you may find great success implementing your serverless MapReduce system, there are alternatives that still fall under the serverless umbrella or leverage managed services, which should give you a high degree of confidence. I'll talk through some of the other systems or techniques you should consider when working on your own data analysis.

AWS Athena

AWS Athena is a relatively new service from AWS. Of course, this is specific to AWS, but other cloud providers may offer comparable services. Athena gives you the ability to write SQL queries to analyze data stored on S3. Before you can analyze your data with SQL, you must create a virtual *database* with associated *tables* across your structured or semi-structured S3 files. You may create these tables manually or with another AWS service called **Glue**.

I won't go into all of the details of setting up a new Athena database or tables but will show you the results and ease of use after you've set those up. In this example, I've created a database and table for web server logs from the **Big Data Benchmark** dataset.

 This data is publicly accessible on S3, and the details may be found at the Big Data Benchmark website: `https://amplab.cs.berkeley.edu/benchmark/`

Following is a screenshot from the AWS Athena console. As you can see on the left, I've loaded up my `uservisits` table, which merely points to the public S3 bucket for the `uservisits` log data. I've already created a table so that Athena knows the structure and datatypes for the CSV data stored on S3. Once this is done, I can use ANSI-SQL queries to analyze the data. In the following screenshot, you can see how I've selected the first 10 rows:

It's also possible to rename columns to something meaningful and change datatypes for each column. In my previous example table, several columns are named `colX`, where I've renamed other columns `ip`, `score`, and `agent`.

From there, I'll run a query that calculates the total score grouped by IP address. This query and the results can be seen in the following screenshot:

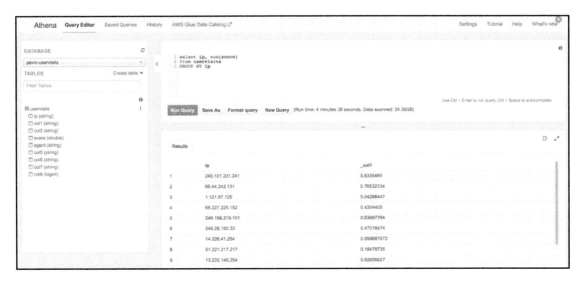

The final results of this query were quite impressive in my opinion. The query scanned just over 24 GB of data on S3 and took just under five minutes to execute. I can view this metadata in the **History** area of Athena:

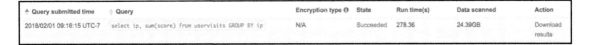

Given the simplicity of the Athena system, it's one that I would strongly suggest you investigate. What is nice about this is that new data may arrive on S3 at regular intervals, and your queries would reflect the results whenever they're run. Additionally, the overhead and price for running these queries are quite low. Anything you can do with ANSI-SQL is possible with Athena. However, Athena has limitations in that your data needs to be well structured and the data prepared ahead of time. In our example MapReduce application, we had application logic that was extracting the To and From fields from email text. To do this with Athena would require a data preparation step to extract that data from the source data, and then store the extracted and structured information on S3.

Using a data store for results

In our example MapReduce system, we stored the state in S3. That is, every mapper would work on a subset of the dataset, do some initial reduce step, and then save the intermediate results as a file on S3. This technique is helpful since it's relatively simple and storing static data on S3 is painless. Since each mapper is writing a unique file to S3, we also didn't have to worry much about race conditions or other mappers overwriting our data.

The downside of this technique is that our reducer needs to read in all of the intermediate results to do the final reduce step. As I explained earlier, this *could* be a limiting factor for your system depending on the size of the final result. One alternative implementation would be using a data store such as Redis to store the mapper keys and values.

The way this would work is that mappers, working in parallel, would process subsets of the initial dataset. Once the mappers have finished their initial aggregation, they would write the results to Redis, which would act as a central location for all of the reduced data. Mappers would either insert new records for a particular key if that key did not exist or update the data for a key. In some cases, such as counting items, we wouldn't even need a reducer as the mappers would merely increment the value stored in Redis if the key was already present.

In cases where we would like to calculate an average or something else that depends on keeping track of all values for a particular key, the reduce step would consist of scanning through all keys and performing the final reduce step based on the values stored for each key.

Imagine a case where we were calculating the average value per key. Mappers would perform work that looked something along these lines:

```
results = {}

for key, value in input_data.items():
    if key not in results:
        results[key] = [value]
    else:
        results[key].append(value)

r = redis.StrictRedis()

# Use a pipeline to ensure we don't hit a race condition
p = r.pipeline()
for key, values in results.items():
    p.lpush(key, *values)
p.execute()
```

Making sure to use the `pipeline` technique to ensure we don't hit a race condition, our mappers push results into Redis as lists for each key. Reducers would then iterate around all of the keys and perform a count of the number of items in each list, as well as summing up the entire list. For example, the average value for a particular key named `height` would look like the following:

```
l = len(r.lrange('height', 0, -1))
avg_height = sum((float(i) for i in r.lrange('height', 0, -1))) / l
```

While Redis is incredibly performant, it would still be easy to overwhelm a single Redis server with enough concurrency from serverless functions. The Redis (or another data store) technique could also be a good workaround for cases when you reach memory limitation in your serverless MapReduce systems. There are other things to consider too, such as, how do you finally report the entire result set in aggregate, if needed. Also, how or when do you clear out the Redis DB?

Using Elastic MapReduce

Elastic MapReduce (EMR) from AWS is another alternative if you need the full power of Hadoop. EMR is just what it sounds like, a managed Hadoop system that is easy to scale up or down as required. The advantage of EMR is that Hadoop developers should feel comfortable since it is a managed Hadoop infrastructure on demand. EMR can also run other frameworks, such as Spark and Hive.

EMR doesn't fit with the *serverless* theme really, since you pay for every minute that a cluster is up, regardless of whether it's running any of your jobs. Still, the fact that you can have a fully-managed Hadoop cluster is quite attractive if your use cases warrant it. Another beautiful thing about EMR, as with all things cloud, is that it's possible to create a cluster on-demand, run your jobs, and then shut it down. Creating and destroying an EMR cluster requires some form of automation with API calls, CloudFormation, or Terraform, but it's still possible and the more automation you can put in place, the better.

Summary

In this chapter, I gave an overview of what the MapReduce pattern looked like in a general sense and demonstrated how MapReduce works with some example code. From there, we reviewed the MapReduce pattern as applied to serverless architectures. We stepped through the details of implementing this pattern by parsing 1.5 GB of email data and counting the unique occurrences of From and To email addresses. I showed that a serverless system could be built using this pattern to perform our task in less than a minute, on average.

We covered some of the limitations of this pattern when implemented on a serverless platform. Finally, we discussed alternative solutions for general data analysis problems using serverless platforms such as AWS Athena and managed systems such as EMR, as well as ways to use a centralized data store such as Redis in a serverless MapReduce system.

Deployment and CI/CD Patterns

9

One of the big advantages of serverless architectures is the ease, speed, and agility with which you can develop and deploy your application. While the various serverless frameworks out there give you tools to manage your application's lifecycle, there are still many questions to answer when it comes to managing deployments and environments. Additionally, the question of unit tests is sometimes more difficult to answer since serverless architectures often use managed services such as databases, queues, and the like.

In this chapter, you will learn deployment tooling, techniques, and considerations. We will also discuss **continuous integration (CI)** and **continuous delivery (CD)** systems and how they hook into unit testing and automated deployments.

By the end of this chapter, you will have learned the following:

- Deployment options and techniques for serverless applications
- The landscape of CI/CD systems and how they work with serverless applications
- General best practices in setting up serverless application code for unit testing
- How to set up unit tests for a serverless Python REST application using Docker
- How to set up CI with CircleCI to run unit tests and report test coverage on each commit
- How to set up CI with CircleCI to deploy our production application for every commit to the `production` branch when tests pass

Introduction to CI/CD

CI and CD are often grouped in discussions around software development life cycles or software engineering best practices. However, CI and CD are distinct concepts with their own sets of best practices, challenges, and goals. This section will not attempt to cover the broad subject of CI and CD, but it is essential to talk about a few concepts and ideas to have a discussion that applies to serverless architectures and systems.

Most of these ideas were born out of the Agile and **Extreme Programming** (**XP**) communities. While these are not hard rules that every team needs to follow, they do come from groups of people who were looking to solve real-world problems. Adopting these practices can help any team and any project, whether the project is serverless or not.

CI

CI is the process of merging code changes into a mainline branch (for example, often a `master` branch if using Git) early and often. Before a merge from a development branch to a master branch, some preconditions should be met:

1. Unit tests must be run and pass
2. New tests must cover the newly added code
3. Another team member must do a code review or be the result of a pair programming session

In a serverless system, there aren't many special considerations when talking about CI. Pair programming, unit testing, and test coverage are ideas that are not unique to any particular architecture. However, there are a few tricks to setting up serverless application code that make testing easier and even fun. I'll discuss some specific scenarios and tips in the *Setting up unit tests* section.

CD

While CI is usually easily understood, I feel that CD is often conflated with continuous deployment. Traditional CD is the process of building, testing and releasing software rapidly. Since *testing* is wrapped up in this definition, there is, of course, a natural relationship with CI. I view CD more on the spectrum of setting up automated systems so that the process of fixing a bug and deploying that fix safely and reliably to production is as fast and easy to hand off as possible.

Continuous deployment is a particular feature wrapped up within CD, that is, every merge to the production branch results in a deployment to the production system. A good CD pipeline enables continuous deployments, but it's up to the team behind the software whether or not to enable or use continuous deployment. More specifically, continuous deployment requires CD, but just because a good CD system is in place does not mean that the team is utilizing continuous deployment.

A good CD system may look like the following:

1. Teammates pair program to implement a feature on a branch named `feature/xyx`
2. The code is checked in, and CI system runs unit tests and code coverage
3. The team is notified of test results and given code coverage results
4. Team merges `feature/xyz` branch to `master` branch
5. Tests are rerun on the `master` branch
6. The team is informed of test results on the `master` branch
7. `master` branch code is automatically deployed to production

Again, it's up to the team whether the final step of automatic deployment occurs or not. However, the entire CD pipeline should be set up so that it's *possible*. When you set up a CD pipeline to *enable* continuous deployments, you'll have solved most of the hard problems, which makes your software development life cycle that much faster and more efficient.

Like CI, serverless systems look mostly the same as traditional software systems when it comes to CD. One nice thing here is that the serverless frameworks give us tooling to perform deployments. In non-serverless systems, deployment scripts are often left as exercises for teams to undertake using a myriad of tooling, the choices of which are vast and not always obvious. In the serverless landscape, deployment options are usually limited by your framework of choice.

Setting up unit tests

As I mentioned in the prior section, there are a few tricks and tips in setting up unit tests with a serverless system. The most important thing you can do is completely isolate your application code from the fact that it is running in a serverless context or within a given cloud provider. This strategy will lend other significant benefits other than making our tests easier to run, and I'll discuss those advantages in the course of this discussion on testing.

Code organization

What does our code layout look like when we attempt to isolate application code from cloud provider-specific code? Let's take a look at the following diagram that shows the high-level structure of our REST or GraphQL API from Chapter 2, *A Three-Tier Web Application Using REST*, and Chapter 3, *A Three-Tier Web Application Pattern with GraphQL*, respectively:

`Makefile`	Helper

`handler.py`
or
`handler.js`
	Main entrypoint, contains cloud provider specific code

`lib/`
or
`node_packages/`
	Installed libraries

`cupping/`	Application code with all business logic. No provider-specific code or logic.
`tests/`	Unit tests

Our example application was authored in Python, but this diagram shows how this general code organization can work for Node, Python, or any other language. In addition to being language-agnostic, this should be both framework- and cloud provider-agnostic. The primary goal of this layout is to isolate your application code from any vendor, framework, or other third-party systems.

The main ideas behind this code organization are the following:

- The primary handler or entry point that is invoked by the cloud provider contains any cloud-specific code and bootstraps the rest of the code (for instance, managing paths if necessary).
- Any additional libraries are wrapped up alongside the handler file.

- Tests are isolated in a `tests` directory. Only testing-related code goes in here, including mocks or factories.
- All application logic is namespaced within a separate directory (`cupping`, in this example).

With this setup, there are several advantages and no obvious disadvantages:

- If you ever decide to change cloud providers, no application code changes are necessary. The only changes needed would be in the `handler` file.
- Tests are wholly isolated from application code and are not deployed with application code.
- The structure is very trim and easy to navigate and understand for other developers.
- If any path manipulation is needed to find packages (as is the case with Python) you only need to add a single directory to the runtime path.
- It is trivial to point any test runner at the single `tests` directory to run unit tests.

Anyone writing serverless functions with Node shouldn't need to deal with system paths explicitly, as is necessary for Python. Node.js will automatically resolve `node_modules` as you'd expect. Some of these tips are therefore applicable only to Python developers or those using other supported languages that don't resolve libraries via convention.

Setting up unit tests

With `py.test`, a single file named `conftest.py` controls testing setup and configuration. If you can remember back to our discussion on setting up the runtime in `handler.py`, we had a few lines of code that added `lib` to our system path, which is shown in the following code. The next code block is taken directly from our `handler.py` function:

```
from pathlib import Path

# Munge our sys path so libs can be found
CWD = Path(__file__).resolve().cwd() / 'lib'
sys.path.insert(0, str(CWD))
```

When we run our tests using `py.test`, the main entry point will be our test code rather than `handler.py`. As such, any bootstrapping of our code needs to take place in a different location since `handler.py` will not always be imported before every test. In a testing context, `conftest.py` is the new entry point where any system bootstrapping and configuration will occur. In addition to managing our system path, which will now be relative to the `tests/` directory, our `conftest.py` file will also be responsible for setting up environment variables that were previously managed by our serverless framework stack. The following code from `conftest.py` shows the path manipulation and environment variable setup so that our tests can import application code and execute successfully during a test run:

```python
from pathlib import Path

CWD = Path(__file__).resolve().parent
code_dir = CWD / '../serverless'
lib_dir = CWD / '../serverless/lib'

sys.path.append(str(code_dir))
sys.path.append(str(lib_dir))

ENV = os.environ['ENV']
os.environ.update({
    'CUPPING_DB_PASSWORD': '',
    'CUPPING_DB_USERNAME': 'postgres',
    'CUPPING_DB_HOST': 'cupping-%s-postgres' % ENV,
})

if os.environ.get('CIRCLECI'):
    os.environ['CUPPING_DB_HOST'] = 'localhost'
```

Our test code will need to import two different types of code:

- Our application code
- Third-party packages

With this being the case, we need to add two directories to our system path. The first path we add to the system path (`code_dir`) corresponds to the location of our application code. The second path we add to the system path (`lib_dir`) corresponds to the directory for third-party libraries. In the previous code block, you can view how that path manipulation is being handled manually.

Next, we'll need to manage environment variables. In this project, there aren't many to contend with. All of the above environment variables deal with our PostgreSQL database, which happens to be running as a linked Docker container. You'll notice in the final `if` statement there is a check for an environment variable named `CIRCLECI`. If that is present, this setup code will change the host variable for our PostgreSQL database. I'll review this in more detail in the following section.

Setting up CI with CircleCI

There is a reasonably extensive landscape when it comes to hosted CI systems. If you add in self-hosted systems, the list grows even longer. Tools such as Jenkins have been around for many years, initially as self-hosted systems. Inevitably, hosted versions of tools such as Jenkins have emerged from various companies. In this section, we'll walk through the steps of setting up CircleCI (`https://circleci.com`) to run our unit tests and produce a code coverage report on every code commit.

> Since this is a book about serverless patterns, I'll encourage you to pick whatever tool works for your purposes with a very strong lean towards hosted CI/CD system. Using a hosted CI/CD systems means that you can focus more on your application code rather than the CI/CD system, which is just a tool we need to get our jobs done.

Setting up a brand new project with CircleCI is quite simple, and it has easy integration with both GitHub and Bitbucket. The first thing you'll need to do to set up a new project is log in with one of those two services. From there, you can go to the **Projects** item in the left-hand-side navigation menu and click on the **Add Project** button in the upper-right of the screen.

The following screenshot shows this navigation; however, I've already set up this example project, which is the reason it shows up in the list:

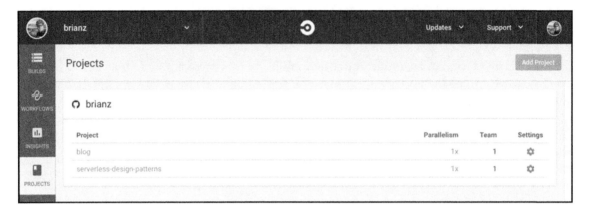

 You can see that I also have my blog set up in CircleCI. CI can be used for any repository where you'd like to perform some automated set of steps when code is committed, or branches are merged. In the case of my blog, a script will deploy any new posts or changes out once they are checked in.

Configuring CircleCI builds

There is a plethora of options and controls that you can configure within CircleCI. There are only a few settings we'll need to control from within the CircleCI web interface. Everything else will be controlled via a `config.yml` configuration file, which we will add to the repository.

Our first step is putting together a `.circleci/config.yml` file. The `.circleci/` directory lives in the root of our repository. The following code block shows the configuration to run unit tests in for our REST API, which is located in the `ch2/` directory of the repository:

```
version: 2
jobs:

  build:
    docker:
      - image: verypossible/serverless:1.25.0-python3
      - image: postgres
    environment:
      - ENV: circleci
```

```
steps:
  - checkout
  - restore_cache:
      key: dependency-cache-{{ checksum "ch2/requirements.txt" }}
  - run:
      name: Install python requirements
      working_directory: ch2
      command: make libs
  - save_cache:
      key: dependency-cache-{{ checksum "ch2/requirements.txt" }}
      paths:
        - ch2/lib
  - run:
      name: py.test
      working_directory: ch2
      command: make tests
  - store_artifacts:
      path: ch2/htmlcov/
      destination: coverage
```

 There is some extra work involved in this setup since our application code lives in the `ch2/` directory but commands always start from the root directory. In a regular repository where the code isn't contained in a subdirectory, dealing with the `working_directory` would be unnecessary.

CircleCI 2.0 uses Docker containers for their builds. What this means for us is that it's quite easy to pull in any additional resources our application code may need to run tests. In this case, we'll pull in the official `postgres` Docker image. Another benefit of this is that I use a Docker container for building libraries, running tests, and doing deployments. Since all of this functionality is possible using the `verypossible/serverless` images, which I built, we can just use the same image to run these tests and do deployments as we did during development. The first image listed under the `docker` key previously will be the primary container where the code will be checked out, and any commands will run.

The Docker image and Makefile that I'm using here are set up to use a variable named `ENV`. I'll set the `ENV` variable in this configuration file. After the environment section begins, a list of steps that run in sequence and make up the actual test run. The steps to set up and run the tests consist of:

1. Check out code
2. Restore cache, so that the supporting packages are only downloaded when there is a change
3. Install supporting packages, in case they are not cached

4. Save cache
5. Run unit tests with the `make tests` command
6. Store test coverage results, so they are viewable on CircleCI

> A few different commands deal with saving and restoring the cache. These cache controls are specific to CircleCI, and I encourage you to read about it in detail in the CircleCI docs. At a high level, these steps are saving some CPU cycles by caching any installed libraries from previous runs rather than doing package downloads and installs for every test run.

There are two `run` directives, which perform the bulk of the work. Both `Install Python requirements` and `py.test` steps use `make` targets to do their work. We've already set up the actual logic of what those commands do, which you can review by inspecting the Makefile. Neither of these commands is incredibly complex (installing packages and running test). Since we've already done this work of wrapping up the details in the Makefile, we can take advantage of these and other make shortcuts.

Finally, after tests are run, I'll set up CircleCI to upload the test coverage output files to the build's artifacts. Build artifacts are another CircleCI-specific task, although I know other CI systems have something similar. After the HTML coverage output is uploaded as a CircleCI artifact, we'll be able to view the results via the CircleCI website.

The following screenshot shows all of the `coverage` output files listed in the **Artifacts** tab for each build:

Since the coverage report is created in HTML format, I can click on the `index.html` file to see the complete test results. The following screenshot shows the test coverage report after I clicked on `index.html`:

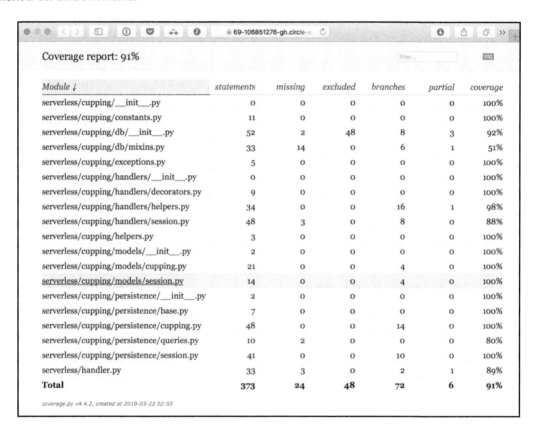

Setting up environment variables

Earlier in this chapter, you'll remember that there were some environment variables that we needed to take care of in our tests. Additionally, there was a small switch in our `conftest.py` file that set the PostgreSQL host based on the presence of a particular environment variable. CircleCI is kind enough to inject a couple of environment variables during a build, one of which is named `CIRCLECI`. Using this variable, we'll update the database host during test runs, which happens to be `localhost`. When we're testing our code locally with Docker containers that we manage, the hostname will be that of our linked PostgreSQL container.

In addition to handling specific environment variables differently when running within a CircleCI build, we'll also need to manage any sensitive variables in preparation for deployments. Because those variables relate to the deployment of our stack, I'll cover this in the next section about continuous deployment.

Setting up CD and deployments with CircleCI

As I mentioned in the introductory section of this chapter, the **D** in **CD** stands for **Delivery**. In this section, we'll walk through the details of setting up both delivery and deployment of our application via CircleCI. I will admit, the boundaries here between delivery and deployment are a bit blurred, and any such discussions can become difficult due to disagreements in terminology and details. For our purposes, our CD pipeline will focus on the following:

- Visibility
- Feedback
- Ease of automated deployments

For visibility and feedback, we'll use Slack and GitHub badges. Our existing deployment script from the Makefile and the serverless framework will be hooked into CircleCI to make production deployments fast, simple, and reliable.

Setting up Slack notifications

CircleCI has several integrations with various chat systems. Setting up test results to be posted to Slack (or your messaging platform of choice) is a straightforward and effective way to disseminate test results among team members.

In CircleCI, navigate to the **Chat Notifications** menu item and click on the link in the **Slack** section. From there, you'll be guided through the setup process for you Slack group. Ultimately, you'll get a webhook URL from Slack, which you will need to enter into CircleCI. Notification will be sent to this Slack webhook, which will post to a particular channel.

The following screenshot shows project settings for this repository within CircleCI and the page where you configure chat notifications:

After tests run, you'll see the results show up in Slack. The following two screenshots show success and failure messages in Slack, delivered by CircleCI:

If tests fail, the message will look slightly different. The following shows the message when tests fail from another project I work on:

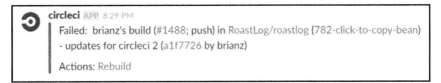

Setting up a CircleCI badge

Current test results can also be displayed in markdown files. This badge is especially useful in GitHub or Bitbucket README files. In the **Notifications** | **Status Badges** section of CircleCI, you can find a markdown (or another format) snippet, which you can copy and put into your README.md file.

After putting that CircleCI-generated markdown snippet into the README.md file, GitHub will display the current status of the last build, as shown in the following screenshot:

Serverless REST API

This is an example project of a serverless REST API using the Serverless Framework. This project corresponds to Chapter 2 of Serverless Design Patterns and Best Practices

[PASSED]

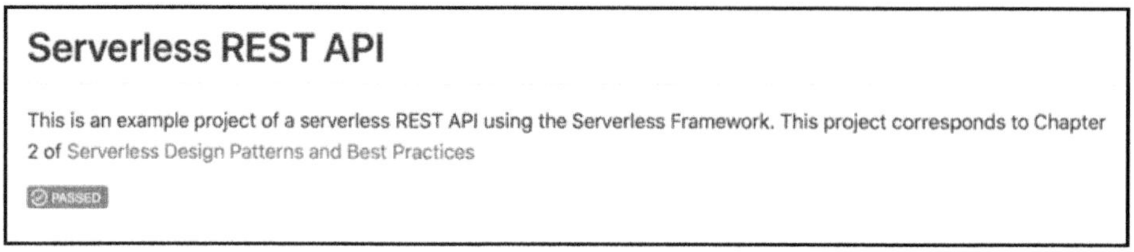

Setting up deployments

We now have our tests running automatically, as well as notifications about test results being pushed to Slack. Now, we can work on getting CircleCI to deploy our code to AWS for us automatically. I'll be working through the steps to enable automated deployments. You may not want to do automated deployments for each of your projects. However, you should work toward being *able* to perform continuous deployments. Even if you choose not to release production code like this, working toward continuous deployment as an end goal means that you will have automated the majority of your build pipeline.

Setting up AWS credentials

Using AWS credentials is such a common task that CircleCI has a special section for it in each project's configuration. If you navigate to **Permissions** | **AWS Permissions,** you'll find two fields for your AWS Access Key ID and AWS Secret Key. Setting these here ensures you'll never need to check them into source control and that any AWS libraries you use (noted in the following screenshot) will automatically pick up the values as environment variables.

Setting these credentials in this section works as we would expect for the Serverless framework, allowing any `serverless` command to execute successfully provided the keys we attach have the correct IAM permissions:

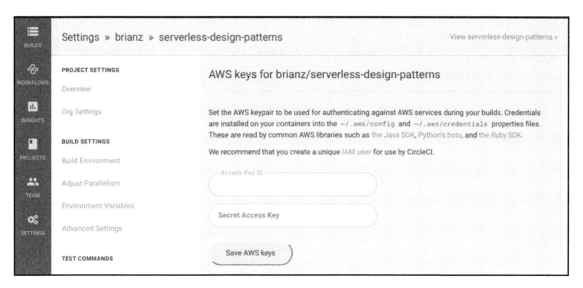

Setting up environment variables

Some of the non-critical variables, such as the test database host and username, are easy to deal with in code or configuration files that are tracked in version control (such as `.circleci/config.yml`). When we turn our attention to deployments, however, there are inevitably variables that you would prefer to keep secret and never check into version control.

In cases like this, we can add variables via CircleCI from the **Build Settings | Environment Variables** section. In the following screenshot, you can see how I'm setting the database password for the PostgreSQL RDS instance:

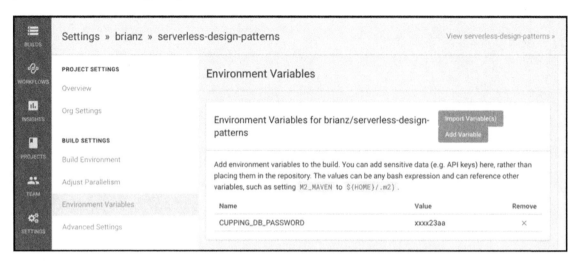

As a quick review of how this entire system works, variables from the environment are picked up by the Serverless framework. In the case of some of the RDS variables, we inject the values into our Lambda functions via serverless and use the variables when creating and setting up an RDS instance. The related snippets of `serverless.yml` are as follows:

```
provider:
  environment:
    CUPPING_DB_USERNAME: ${env:CUPPING_DB_USERNAME}
    CUPPING_DB_PASSWORD: ${env:CUPPING_DB_PASSWORD}
    CUPPING_DB_NAME: ${env:CUPPING_DB_NAME}

resources:
  Resources:
    RDSPostgresInstance:
      Type: AWS::RDS::DBInstance
      Properties:
        DBName: ${env:CUPPING_DB_NAME}
        MasterUsername: ${env:CUPPING_DB_USERNAME}
        MasterUserPassword: ${env:CUPPING_DB_PASSWORD}
```

Any value we set in CircleCI for the `CUPPING_DB_PASSWORD` will be available during any `serverless` commands we execute from within CircleCI.

Executing deployments

With all of the setup out of the way, we can update our CircleCI configuration to deploy code on our behalf. During the CI tasks, we utilized our various `make` targets to perform work that we were already doing manually. For deployments, we'll reuse another pre-existing `make` target that is already set up, `make deploy`.

Under the `jobs` key, we'll add another step named `deploy`, which comes after our build step. This new deploy job has the same configuration options available as the previous build step. Our goal in this deploy step is actually to perform the deployment out to our production environment. For that to work, there are different configuration options that we'll need to set up, the details of which you can see in the following YAML snippet from `.circleci/config.yml`.

With CircleCI, each section under the jobs keys is a standalone body of work, which you may define and configure on its own. These steps can work together or in parallel, as we'll see shortly. In this case, we already have a `build/test` section, and we're now adding a `deploy` section. These two jobs will work together, so our code is deployed only after tests are run and pass.

We'll be using the same Docker image to perform our deployments, which you can see in the image section. For our deployments to work, some environment variables need to exist, as I mentioned earlier in this chapter. Here, we can set up those variables in our configuration file. The RDS password is missing from this list on purpose since it will be injected into our deployment phase by CircleCI because we defined it from the CircleCI web application. Finally, the steps for deploying our Serverless project are as follows:

1. Check out code
2. Run `make libs` from the `ch2` directory
3. Run `make deploy` from the `ch2` directory

The following code block shows the `deploy` step of `.circleci/config.yml` as well as the workflows, that chains together tests and deployments:

```
jobs:

  build:
    # build steps

  deploy:
    docker:
      - image: verypossible/serverless:1.25.0-python3
```

```
    environment:
      - ENV: production
      - AWS_REGION: us-west-2
      - VPC_ID: vpc-abc12345
      - SUBNET_ID_A: subnet-11111111
      - SUBNET_ID_B: subnet-22222222
      - SUBNET_ID_C: subnet-33333333
      - CUPPING_DB_USERNAME: root
      - CUPPING_DB_NAME: cupping_log
    steps:
      - checkout
      - run:
          name: Build libs
          working_directory: ch2
          command: make libs
      - run:
          name: Production deploy if tests pass and branch is
production
          working_directory: ch2
          command: make deploy

workflows:
  version: 2
  build-deploy:
    jobs:
      - build
      - deploy:
          requires:
            - build
          filters:
            branches:
              only: production
```

 These job keys can be named anything you like and make sense to you. I happened to name them `build` and `deploy`. However, I could have called them `test` and `deploy`, or `build-test` and `rollout`.

With our deploy steps defined, we can instruct CircleCI to do our deployment under certain conditions via their workflows feature. The full capabilities of this feature are vast, but in our case the goal is simple; we want to do the deployment only when we are on the `production` branch and when tests have passed. You can see all of this logic in the `workflows` section in the previous configuration.

To see this in action, I performed the following steps:

1. Checked in some changes to the `feature/circleci` branch
2. Created a GitHub pull request against the `production` branch
3. Merged the pull request

> Very often a deployment flow such as this will work off the `master` branch. Here, I've chosen to use a branch named `production`. This change in naming convention is because this book's repository may have several commits for the various chapters and I don't want every commit to `master` to trigger a CircleCI `build-deploy` workflow.

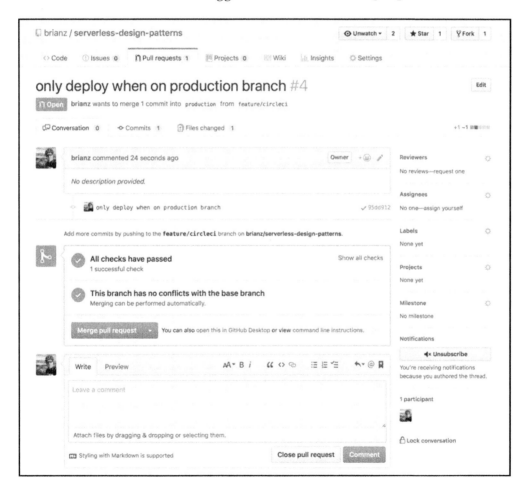

The previous screenshot shows the pull request details. With CircleCI set up, any pull request will show the details of the test run. Here, we can see our tests have successfully run. I also received a Slack notification of the successful tests.

Once I click **Merge pull request**, another CircleCI build begins. In the following screenshot you can see that, because the `production` branch was updated, our `build-deploy` workflow is running:

After the build job runs and tests pass, the deploy step will commence. We can see this in CircleCI with their workflows visualization, shown in the following screenshot:

By clicking on the **deploy** box, we can watch or see the details of the `deploy` phase:

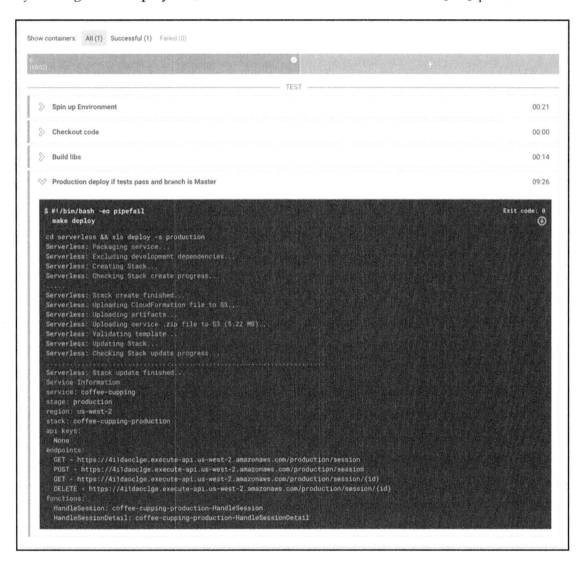

Success! Since our `make deploy` command works for creating a brand new stack or updating an existing one, there is nothing more we need to do from here on. Any merges or commits to our `production` branch will trigger this flow, and we now have continuous deployment working.

Summary

In this chapter, we reviewed the meaning and high-level details of CI and CD. I also discussed some best practices on how to organize application code in serverless projects to help set up and run unit tests. From there, I covered how to set up our unit tests to run on every commit using CircleCI.

Finally, we worked through the entire process of setting up CircleCI to perform automated deployments triggered by changes to the `production` branch. You learned some of the nuances of controlling CI execution via environment variables and where to configure sensitive settings such as database passwords and AWS keys.

10
Error Handling and Best Practices

Serverless architectures are different enough that techniques and best practices need to be thought through and evaluated to be successful. Many traditional methods for debugging, application development, monitoring, and so on are still applicable in a server-based architecture. However, many tried-and-tested techniques that you may rely on when working with virtual machines or real hardware will not necessarily work with serverless systems. When building on top of a FaaS platform, then, you need to keep these differences in mind and have a plan for monitoring, debugging, testing, and developing your serverless application.

In this chapter, we'll review common best practices that will help you to focus on building your application rather than getting stuck in the details of organization or deployment. We'll also cover the tools and methods available for keeping your serverless application secure, easy to develop locally, and observable. We'll also discuss the changes you will need to make to track errors and monitor serverless applications reliably.

It's worth noting here that one could dedicate an entire book to best practices for serverless applications. This chapter is not exhaustive by any means, but it will cover many topics which will definitely help to improve your serverless development experience and the overall quality of your application.

By the end of this chapter, you can expect to understand the following topics:

- How to set up your application to track unexpected errors with Sentry and Rollbar
- Working with cold starts
- Monitoring and alerting around errors, exceptions, or performance degradation
- Local development and testing
- How to manage configuration via environment variables across different stacks (development versus production)
- How to encrypt sensitive environment variables to keep your application secure

Error tracking

Practically speaking, all software systems crash at some point. One of the reasons I love working with serverless systems so much is that they, by their very nature, keep an application relatively small and more akin to a microservice, rather than a broad monolithic application. This fact by itself can drastically reduce the number of ways an application can fail. However, at some point, it will fail, and an exception you didn't expect will occur. What, then, is the best way to handle unexpected exceptions in a serverless system?

The good news here is that we have multiple options, and that some systems you may already be familiar with can work in the same way as they would in a non-serverless system. In the following sections, we'll walk through the steps for integrating two popular error tracking services, Sentry and Rollbar. Both services offer similar functionality and are equally easy to set up. In the following examples, we'll be using Python, but both Sentry and Rollbar support a myriad of languages including Node.js, Java, Golang, and C#.

Integrating Sentry for error tracking

I have used Sentry for many years and highly recommend it. It has a vast feature set and many prominent companies use the service. Sentry's free plan gives you 10,000 events per month, a single login, and a seven-day history of quickly. Whether it's for a hobby project or even a medium-scale production system, this free plan works out quite well.

To integrate Sentry with your serverless function, you'll, of course, need a Sentry account. Following is a code block for an elementary AWS Lambda function. All it will do is calculate the quotient of two numbers. Our goal is to ensure that any unhandled exceptions are captured and reported somewhere so that we have visibility into what our application is doing and have as much information as possible with which to debug it:

```python
def divide(event, context):
    params = event.get('queryStringParameters') or {}
    numerator = int(params.get('numerator', 10))
    denominator = int(params.get('denominator', 2))
    body = {
        "message": "Results of %s / %s = %s" % (
            numerator,
            denominator,
            numerator // denominator,
        )
    }

    response = {
        "statusCode": 200,
        "body": json.dumps(body)
    }

    return response
```

We've set this up with API Gateway, so we can execute it using `curl` and get results for two numbers, as shown in the following snippet:

```
$ curl
"https://5gj9zthyv1.execute-api.us-west-2.amazonaws.com/dev?numerator=12&de
nominator=3"
{"message": "Results of 12 / 3 = 4"}
```

Let's see what happens when we divide this by 0, which we know is undefined in mathematics:

```
$ curl
"https://5gj9zthyv1.execute-api.us-west-2.amazonaws.com/dev?numerator=10&de
nominator=0"
{"message": "Internal server error"}
```

As an application developer, I have no way of knowing that this error has occurred as there is no monitoring in place. The only way I can know that an error has happened is if I log into the AWS console and look at the execution metrics for my Lambda function, or if I happen to be reading through the CloudWatch Logs. Of course, you can't be manually watching for errors day and night. The following screenshot shows **Invocation errors** from the AWS Lambda monitoring page for the `divide` function:

AWS CloudWatch chart from the Lambda screen, showing a count of the number of errors

CloudWatch will capture `stdout` and `stderr` for Lambda functions. Because unhandled exceptions are written to `stderr`, we can see the details when looking at the CloudWatch logs, as shown in the following screenshot:

```
▶   23:17:17              START RequestId: d961abdd-1e6f-11e8-ade7-418e88b21bc5 Version: $LATEST
▼   23:17:17              integer division or modulo by zero: ZeroDivisionError Traceback (most recent call last):

integer division or modulo by zero: ZeroDivisionError
Traceback (most recent call last):
File "/var/task/lib/raven_python_lambda/__init__.py", line 197, in decorated
raise e
File "/var/task/lib/raven_python_lambda/__init__.py", line 194, in decorated
return fn(event, context)
File "/var/task/handler.py", line 29, in divide
numerator // denominator,
ZeroDivisionError: integer division or modulo by zero


▶   23:17:17              END RequestId: d961abdd-1e6f-11e8-ade7-418e88b21bc5
▶   23:17:17              REPORT RequestId: d961abdd-1e6f-11e8-ade7-418e88b21bc5 Duration: 364.44 ms
```

AWS CloudWatch logs, showing an unhandled exception due to division by zero

Integrating Sentry will capture unexpected errors, store them, and notify us via various delivery mechanisms. Getting Sentry reporting for our Lambda functions is quite easy. For Python, you can use the `raven-python-lambda` (https://github.com/Netflix-Skunkworks/raven-python-lambda) library and add a decorator around handler functions, as shown in the following snippet:

```
from raven_python_lambda import RavenLambdaWrapper

@RavenLambdaWrapper()
def divide(event, context):
    # Code
```

The only other bit of configuration we need to take care of here is setting the Sentry DSN, which tells the library where to send its payload when an error occurs. Doing this is it's just a matter of passing the values from the host system's environment variables into the Lambda function's environment variables. Using the Serverless Framework, this is quite easy, as you can see:

```
provider:
  name: aws
  runtime: python3.6
  region: ${env:AWS_REGION}
  state: ${env:$ENV}
  environment:
    SENTRY_ENVIRONMENT: ${env:ENV}
    SENTRY_DSN: ${env:SENTRY_DSN}
```

Now Sentry will capture any unhandled exceptions and, at a minimum, email them to us. In the following screenshot, you can see a list of various exceptions. What is neat is that some of these errors were not even deliberate. As you can see in the last row, I misspelled a variable name which caused my division calculation to throw an error:

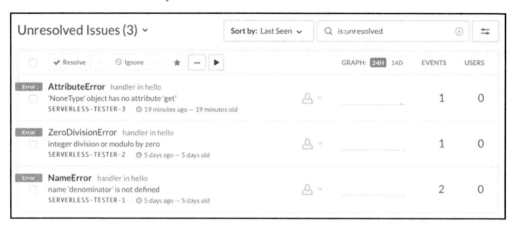

Clicking on any of these errors gives us more context into the state of our application when the exception was triggered, as shown in the following screenshot:

Another lovely feature of the `raven-python-lambda` library is that it will raise warnings when your function is getting too close to its timeout value or its maximum allocated memory. To test this, we need to set the timeout of the `divide` function to 4 seconds and put `time.sleep(3)` in the middle of the application code. After executing the divide Lambda function, you should get a result as expected. You will also receive an email about the slow execution speed and see the same warning on the Sentry website, as shown in the following screenshot:

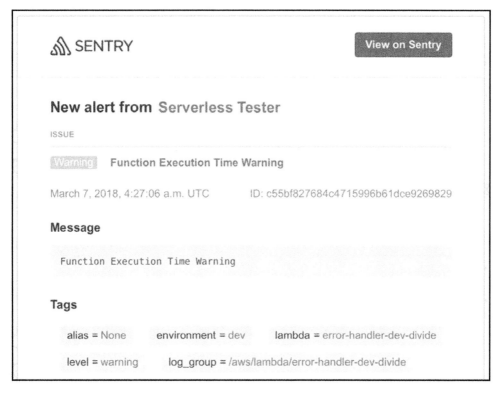

There is much more information included with each exception to help you while debugging on the Sentry website. There are also many more features in Sentry that we don't have room for here; however, a few features worth noting are as follows:

- Chat integration (Slack, IRC, etc.)
- Tracking deployments
- Issue rollup and status tracking

Integrating Rollbar

Rollbar plays the same role as Sentry. Integration is equally as simple. We will still use a decorator for our handler functions, but we'll need a different library with Rollbar. Rollbar provides an official library for Python (`https://github.com/rollbar/pyrollbar`) and many other languages.

The setup changes slightly with `pyrollbar`, but it's nothing too complicated. The following code block shows how to set up an AWS Lambda function for error tracking with Rollbar.

```
import rollbar

token = os.getenv('ROLLBAR_KEY', 'missing_api_key')
rollbar.init(token, os.getenv('ENV', 'dev'))

@rollbar.lambda_function
def divide(event, context):
    # code
```

When we hit an exception, information is delivered to Rollbar. Again, an email notification about the `ZeroDivisionError` should be received. Just like Sentry, there are plenty of integrations from Rollbar.

The following screenshot shows error details displayed on the Rollbar website:

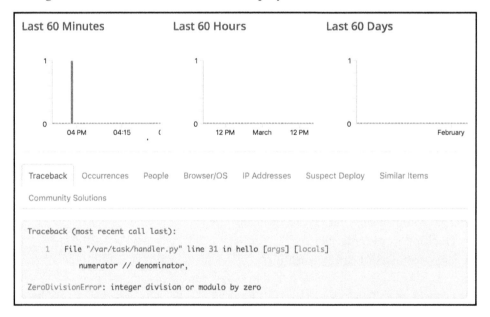

Logging

Tracking exceptions and problems within your application is critical; however, there will inevitably be cases where you wish you had more insight into the state of your application when a problem occurs. For this task, you will need to set yourself up with a good logging strategy. Log messages are a tool we have used for a very long time - and still use often. Very often, log messages are sent to files on disk and then shipped off to a log aggregator. Since we don't have access to these same types of logging system in a serverless architecture, we'll need to come up with something new.

AWS Lambda functions and other FaaS providers offer some mechanisms for keeping track of `stdout` and `stderr` streams. In the case of Lambda, any `print` statements or other error messages will end up in CloudWatch Logs. This delivery to CloudWatch happens automatically, and is especially useful as you'll always know where to go to check for errors or debugging statements. While this is a helpful feature, there are a few improvements we can make to your logging statements so that they're easier to search through, find, and categorize.

Structuring log messages

Log messages are often used as plain strings via `console.log` or `print` statements. These quick and dirty additions to code can be helpful during development but won't suffice in a production-level system. Rather than logging flat strings, log statements need to be structured so that you can easily find the bits of information you're looking for. JSON is an excellent choice for a format since it's widely used among different log aggregator services and easy to implement in practically any language.

Let's take the simple case of our previous divide function. At some point, we may want to understand how people are using our service: specifically, what numerator and denominators they're sending us. To do this, we will need to structure some log messages so that we can quickly search through them, pull out the pertinent information, and finally analyze it. The following code block shows some Python code to bootstrap the `structlog` library. This library will take care of logging structured messages, rather than the flat messages we usually get from the standard library's `logging` module:

```
import structlog
structlog.configure(
        processors=[structlog.processors.JSONRenderer()]
)
log = structlog.get_logger()
```

In our divide function, we can now log any data we find interesting as key-value pairs, shown as follows:

```python
def divide(event, context):
    params = event.get('queryStringParameters') or {}
    log.msg('start', **params)

    numerator = int(params.get('numerator', 10))
    denominator = int(params.get('denominator', 2))

    # do division

    log.msg('finish',
            numerator=numerator,
            denominator=denominator,
            quotient=numerator // denominator)
```

Log messages will now arrive in CloudWatch as JSON-formatted objects rather than Python strings, as shown in the following screenshot:

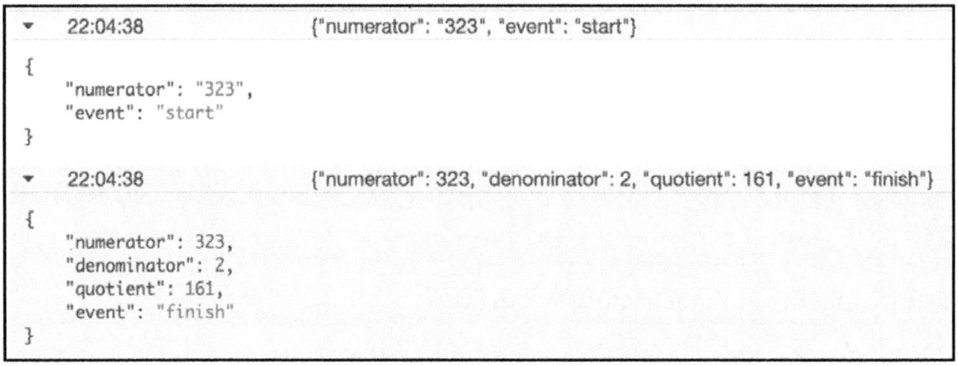

```
▼    22:04:38                     {"numerator": "323", "event": "start"}

{
    "numerator": "323",
    "event": "start"
}

▼    22:04:38                     {"numerator": 323, "denominator": 2, "quotient": 161, "event": "finish"}

{
    "numerator": 323,
    "denominator": 2,
    "quotient": 161,
    "event": "finish"
}
```

This has merely set us up for success; next, we'll work on getting these structured log messages to a log aggregator for better discoverability, analysis, and integration with other services.

Digesting structured logs

Today, there is a myriad of dedicated logging services, such as:

- Loggly
- Sumo Logic
- Splunk
- Papertrail
- Hosted ELK

The list could go on and on. Many of these hosted services may be more accessible, and possibly more powerful, when you send them JSON messages. I have used Loggly in different applications and know that this is the case.

There are many ways to ship logs to Loggly, and likely for other services. However, shipping logs can change when the destination is somewhere other than your FaaS provider. CloudWatch logging is built-in to AWS Lamba and offers free performance, so how can we get these same logs out to an external service?

With AWS CloudWatch, it's possible to trigger another Lambda function when new log messages arrive. That may seem a bit odd, but it's a great trick to keep your application lean and decoupled from any logging service while also solving the problem of getting your log message to a more powerful service. We won't go into all the details on how to set this up here, but there is detailed documentation available on the Loggly site: `https://www.loggly.com/docs/cloudwatch-logs/`.

This pattern is not unique to Loggly in any way. If you are using another logging service and wish to follow the same pattern, it's merely a matter of implementing a Lambda function, which is then triggered by CloudWatch events and sent away to your logging provider of choice.

Once you have JSON messages arriving at your logging provider, you have many more options in terms of data analysis and discovery. Being able to quickly and easily find information when a problem occurs is critical for any production-level system, serverless or not. Regardless of which FaaS or logging service you're using, just make sure that you can easily find the data you need when it's time.

Cold starts

One commonality between most, if not all, FaaS providers is the issue of cold starts. Cold starts are defined as the behavior where an invocation of a cloud function which has not been executed in a while takes a considerable amount of time to initialize before fulfilling the request. If you have used Docker, for example, you'll know that creating a new container from an existing image takes slightly longer than starting up a container you have previously run. This Docker container behavior is analogous to the way cloud functions, whether it be AWS Lambda, Google Cloud Functions, or Azure Cloud Functions, behave. If you do any searching around the internet for serverless cold starts, you'll find several blog posts and documentation on the matter.

There isn't a silver bullet for bypassing the cold start issue. However, there are several things to be aware of so that you can minimize their impact on your application.

Keeping cloud functions warm

There are several tips and tricks you can employ to work around cold starts. The most common recommendation is to implement another function on a timer, say every 5 minutes, which then invokes your target function. With this pattern, the target function is always kept warm, which means it can fulfill a legitimate request more quickly. This can be a useful trick; however, it does not always solve the problem.

Remember, cloud functions will scale automatically. Think back to some of the patterns in this book, specifically the Fanout and MapReduce patterns. In those examples, multiple instances of our functions were being executed concurrently. In the case of our Fanout pattern for image resizing, a single invocation of our initial Lambda function would result in three concurrent image resizing functions. If we had a `ping` function to keep the resizing function active, we would have a single function warm and ready to process that resizing task. However, when three simultaneous invocations occur, a single `ping` function will not help. In this scenario, a single resize function would be warm, but the other two would pay the cold start cost. If we changed our application to resize an image into five different sizes, we would then have four different functions that would start from a *cold* state.

AWS Lambda functions and VPCs

If you are using AWS, keep in mind that cold starts are much worse when running Lambda functions inside a VPC. The reason for this is that Lambda functions in a VPC are allocated an **Elastic Network Interface (ENI)** to access VPC resources such as databases. If you ran the example code `Chapter 2`, *A Three-Tier Web Application Using REST* and `Chapter 3`, *A Three-Tier Web Application Pattern with GraphQL*, you may have noticed that the first API call took several seconds. This initial lag is mainly because the Lambda functions needed access to the RDS instance inside of a VPC, which means the Lambda functions themselves are required to be inside the same VPC.

If at all possible, avoid putting Lambda functions inside a VPC. If your functions do not rely on any external resources, or non-VPC resources such as DynamoDB, do not put them inside of a VPC. However, if you do need access to VPC resources, there aren't many options available. If you are running an API that is talking to a VPC resource such as an RDS instance, you could run a `pinger` function, but we advise raising the concurrency from 1 to something like 10. In this case, you would then have at least 10 functions always warmed up and ready to serve traffic.

Start-up times for different languages

Each supported language comes with its unique behavior in cloud functions. We have not thorough profiled all the different FaaS platforms and languages in this book, but we do know that it has been reported that Node.js and Python have lower cold start times compared with Java and C# on AWS. However, there are also claims that C# functions based on .NET Core 2.0 are significantly faster. AWS recently rolled out support for Golang; however, we are currently unclear on its relative cold start performance.

I may be a bit biased, but I do believe using a language with a lower cold start time is a better choice, at least on AWS, as you can accomplish pretty much anything you need between Node.js and Python. Reading some of the tests people have made, the difference between Java or C# and other languages is two to three orders of magnitude; in other words, cold start times range from 1,000-4,000 ms with Java and C#, whereas Node.js and Python score in the range of 1-10 ms.

Allocating more memory

At least in the case of AWS Lambda, allocating more memory to your functions can result in a faster start-up time. Just as running larger EC2 instances affords you more CPU power, so too does allocating more memory to your Lambda functions. Allocating more memory to your functions may improve performance, but note that this will affect your billing as Lambda functions are billed by the combination of execution duration and allocated memory.

> You can read about CPU allocation relating to AWS Lambda in the following document: `https://docs.aws.amazon.com/lambda/latest/dg/resource-model.html`.

Local development and testing

One challenge we face as serverless engineers is that of convenience. To be more specific, it's a swift process writing code, deploying it, and beginning testing. Testing a live system will often result in some code or configuration issue, but it is quickly fixed and redeployed. The problem we face, therefore, is that it's so easy to fix issues and then redeploy that we can get into the habit of skipping testing or not running our stack locally.

Local development

One question I answer with some regularity is, *How do I run this locally?* When writing a server-based application, one of the first tasks to undertake is getting the system set up so that it can be run during development. When building a serverless-based application, however, there really is no server to run. So, how do we develop our application?

The truthful answer is that this is a challenge, and one that has not been solved perfectly yet; to be fair, this issue is difficult with any microservice-based system. So, how can we run a system and ensure it's fully functional when it's composed of multiple disparate pieces? My belief here is that we need to lean on the principles and strengths of a component-based architecture and use common tools that make local development and testing easier. As you write your serverless application, it's best to focus on the service itself and ensure via unit testing that it works as expected. Don't expect to run a full serverless map-reduce system on your local machine.

In the case of a serverless web API, I rely on unit tests rather than a local server during development. After all, we've long been taught that unit tests are a better approach to development than the manual testing of an API or UI. Regardless of where you stand on that topic, local development of serverless systems can move along quite quickly when writing unit tests, and testing in these systems is relatively simple, as we'll cover in the upcoming section.

 You can read through the repository of community plugins in Serverless Framework here: `https://github.com/serverless/plugins`.

There *are* options for running a serverless application locally, as mentioned previously; however, I have not used these tools myself and cannot speak for the ease or difficulty of using them. For Serverless Framework, however, there are some plugins with the word offline in the name, where the commonality is that they all aim to help you run your application locally. Outside these plugins, DynamoDB has, for a long time, offered an offline version that can be run on your local system.

Serverless systems are still relatively new, and the landscape is maturing and changing quickly. It's almost certain that vendors recognize that there are areas for improvements in the software development lifecycle of serverless applications; I would not be surprised if local development and testing became more comfortable in the coming years.

Learning about testing locally

Concerning local development, I believe the best strategy is to set up robust and thorough unit tests. Unit-testing serverless applications is no different from testing traditional server-based applications. As long as you follow the mantra of keeping your serverless code separate from your business logic, it's quite simple to get to a very high test coverage.

But what do we do when our application relies on backing services such as databases, caches, and the like? Additionally, what do we do when our serverless application calls other services that don't exist locally, such as AWS, SNS, and so on?

My approach to common systems such as Postgres or Redis is to use Docker. If you look back at the unit tests from Chapter 2, *A Three-Tier Web Application Using REST* and Chapter 3, *A Three-Tier Web Application Pattern with GraphQL*, you will see that they rely on a PostgreSQL database. When developing that application, we ran a Docker image that the unit tests used.

Another method for dealing with services you cannot easily run locally or code which *is* focused on serverless-specific logic is the judicious use of mocks. Take, for example, our Messaging Pattern, where our handler function sends messages to SQS. To test this code, we would not want to invoke SQS as that would make our tests slower and they would likely end up brittle. What's better, in this case, is to instead mocking out the API call to SQS and simply test whether the request to the SQS publish function was made.

Likewise, when we want to test some code which is specific to our serverless implementation, mock can come in handy. This is best explained with an example; the following code block shows a single function from our REST API, at the top-level `handler.py` function:

```python
def session_detail(event, context):
    http_method = event['httpMethod']

    status_code = 200
    response = {}

    try:
        response = handle_session_detail(http_method, event)
    except Http404 as e:
        status_code = 404
        response = {'errors': [str(e)]}
    except Exception as e:
        status_code = 500
        response = {'errors': ['Unexpected server error']}

    response = {
        'statusCode': status_code,
        'body': json.dumps(response),
        'headers': CORS_HEADERS,
    }

    return response
```

As you can see, this code has a bit more going on than delegation. Here, the `session_detail` function is catching various errors and setting the HTTP response code and message based on those exceptions, if any are raised. Testing the `handle_session_detail` function is simple, as it is working solely on our application and doesn't contain any reliance on or knowledge of AWS Lambda. However, we do need to test the handling of errors in `session_detail`.

To do this, we use a mock object to patch the `handle_session_detail` method. The aim of the following code block is to trigger an `Http404` exception so that we can verify that the static code and error message are correct. The following code block shows this unit test, where `mocker` is a fixture which comes from the `pytest-mock` library:

```
def test_session_detail_hanlder_404(mocker):
    mock_handler = mocker.patch('handler.handle_session_detail')
    mock_handler.side_effect = Http404('Test 404 error')

    event = {'httpMethod': 'POST'}
    response = handler.session_detail(event, None)
    assert_404(response)
    body = get_body_from_response(response)
    assert body == {'errors': ['Test 404 error']}
    mock_handler.assert_called_once_with('POST', event)
```

Testing is as much an art as it is a science, and so I cannot overstate the importance of testing in serverless applications. As usual, the better your test are, the more confident you'll be when it's time to refactor your code or deploy changes.

Managing different environments

With most production-level applications, teams maintain multiple environments for different purposes. A `QA` environment may exist for the QA team to run automated tests, a `staging` environment may exist for the DevOps team to tests their infrastructure changes, and the `production` environment exists to serve live traffic. Very often, building and maintaining these different environments can be a full-time job.

With serverless systems, I've found that maintaining different environments can be much more straightforward. Some of this may come from the fact that, by their nature, serverless applications are inherently smaller. Writing a monolithic application in a serverless architecture isn't wise - or even natural. How best, then, can we manage and maintain different environments for serverless systems?

For this, turning to tenant III of the 12-Factor App Methodology helps. This tenant can be found at `https://12factor.net/config` and states:

> *Store config in the environment*
> *An app's config is everything that is likely to vary between deploys (staging, production, developer environments, etc.).*

Throughout this book, I used the Serverless Framework to manage and deploy my systems. This framework has built-in support for environment variables, which we can use to our advantage to efficiently manage different systems without making any code changes. The following code block shows a small snippet from the `serverless.yml` file from `Chapter 2`, *A Three-Tier Web Application Using REST* for the coffee cupping REST API:

```
provider:
  name: aws
  runtime: python3.6
  memorySize: 128
  region: ${env:AWS_REGION}
  environment:
    CUPPING_DB_USERNAME: ${env:CUPPING_DB_USERNAME}
    CUPPING_DB_PASSWORD: ${env:CUPPING_DB_PASSWORD}
    CUPPING_DB_NAME: ${env:CUPPING_DB_NAME}
```

Here, any reference to `${env:NAME}` will pull the actual value for `NAME` from the environment. Additionally, Serverless Framework helps us to keep stacks separate by using the `stage` variable to name resources. Whenever deploying code, the deployment step includes the stage variable, which we also pull out of the environment:

```
sls deploy -s $ENV
```

These two techniques combined mean that deploying a `dev` stack or `qa` stack is just a matter of loading different environment variables. You can load environment variables from a file with tools such as `dotenv`, your shell script, or some other tool. My technique uses Docker and a Makefile to load up different variables based on the `ENV` I wish to work with. The result is the same, regardless of how you solve the problem of variable management. If you can quickly change variables, you can easily switch between managing completely different stacks. Remember, if you're using the Serverless Framework you will also need to handle the `ENV` setting. This variable is a single setting which will control the stack that is updated during any deployment.

Securing sensitive configuration

Throughout this book, and in the previous section about managing environments, we've relied heavily on environment variables. One very nice feature of pulling a configuration from the environment is that sensitive information never needs to be checked into the source control. All of our application code and any framework code (such as the Serverless Framework) can look up variable values from the environment when needed.

Configuration via environment variables is all well and good, but our usage of these variables is not perfect. The problem with our usage of environment variables and Lambda is that the data pulled from the deployment environment is uploaded and stored in AWS Lambda functions as plain text. For example, take a look at `serverless.yml` from the previous section about error handling using either Sentry or Rollbar:

```
provider:
  name: aws
  runtime: python3.6
  region: ${env:AWS_REGION}
  state: ${env:$ENV}
  environment:
    SENTRY_ENVIRONMENT: ${env:ENV}
    SENTRY_DSN: ${env:SENTRY_DSN}
    ROLLBAR_KEY: ${env:ROLLBAR_KEY}
```

The keys under the environment key are all set on the AWS Lambda functions. While we never check the values of those variables into source control, they persist inside AWS. In this case, our `SENTRY_DSN` and `ROLLBAR` values should not be shared with anyone. However, if you're working in a team environment, anyone with access to the AWS Lambda console can very easily peek inside your Lambda functions and see the values for any of these variables.

Encrypting variables

To fix this, we can leverage another AWS service called Key Management Service (KMS). KMS works by encrypting data into a string that can only be decrypted using KMS itself. What's nice about using KMS is that you can then store, share, or even check into source control your encrypted variables, since nobody can decrypt them unless they have access to KMS. Your one attack vector here then becomes AWS and KMS itself. If anyone has permission to use your KMS key or can gain access to a privileged AWS account, they can decrypt any KMS-managed variable.

Azure has something similar called Key Vault, which is something you should look into if building on top of Azure. I'm unaware of a similar service within Google Compute or other FaaS providers.

Encrypting data with KMS is quite simple. First, you'll need to create a KMS key. Once you have a key generated you will need to copy the AWS `arn` for your newly created key. From there, you can use a variety of APIs to encrypt a plaintext string. Using the previous example, I'm going to encrypt my DB_PASSWORD of supersecret. The following code block shows how to encrypt a password using Python and the `boto3` library:

```python
import boto3
import base64

key_id = "arn:aws:kms:us-west-2:9802947738:key/fc5753bd-2842-4ff8-
b9a7-61299f4a88c2"
client = boto3.client('kms')

def encrypt():
    stuff = client.encrypt(KeyId=key_id, Plaintext='supersecret')
    binary_encrypted = stuff[u'CiphertextBlob']
    encrypted_password = base64.b64encode(binary_encrypted)
    print("Encrypted password:\n", encrypted_password.decode())
```

The output of this code is an encrypted string, which you can share throughout your infrastructure:

```
Encrypted password:
AQICAHjgjPISkW/L824chyDIq2L43l5kDvqZM/+/CA8zfz94vQGfycexNX4Jq6mbciymbUh
7AAAAaTBnBgkqhkiG9w0BBwagWjBYAgEAMFMGCSqGSIb3DQEHATAeBglghkgBZQMEAS4wEQ
QMymQpnyP3KXAODTaZAgEQgCZ7+oORwCkkT0DUYfILp3Vg1sVGhx0acy1TU2jZAvB54IwrJ
g6cuA==
```

You can accomplish the same task using `aws-cli`, as shown in the following snippet:

```
$ aws kms encrypt --key-id arn:aws:kms:us-
west-2:9802947738:key/fc5753bd-2842-4ff8-b9a7-61299f4a88c2 --plaintext
supersecret
{
    "KeyId": "arn:aws:kms:us-west-2:679892560156:key/cc0e82fe-
bf27-4362-9bf0-292546c81aa8",
    "CiphertextBlob":
"AQICAHjgjPISkW/L824chyDIq2L43l5kDvqZM/+/CA8zfz94vQEON2GSPC5mwzgXBO1bYb4CAA
AAaTBnBgkqhkiG9w0BBwagWjBYAgEAMFMGCSqGSIb3DQEHATAeBglghkgBZQMEAS4wEQQMEuLd/
v+4Hi4M4U6RAgEQgCY1j2xQQG3kRrrSZ2vq0l2uTuQb4GVJTb7pbVd3AbEV7U2HfWGx9A==" 
}
```

Decrypting variables

The question, of course, is how we can use this within our application; the answer is the inverse of what we just did. Now that we have an encrypted variable, our application code will need to read that value and decrypt it. Nothing changes from the standpoint of using environment variables. All that has changed now is that our sensitive variables are no longer stored in plain text anywhere within AWS.

After setting the DB_PASSWORD environment variable to this new encrypted string and redeploying, we can verify that the Lambda console is no longer storing the supersecret password. The following screenshot shows the value for the DB_PASSWORD variable from the AWS Lambda page for my function:

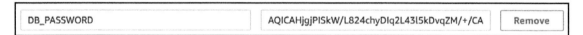

In order for our Lambda functions to use KMS to decrypt this data, we need to authorize it explicitly. To accomplish this, let's add an IAM permission in serverless.yml. In the following snippet, KMs_KEY_ARN is referencing the KMS arn, as explained previously. This value can also be stored as an environment variable which, going back to the section on managing different environments, lets us quickly switch between different stacks where we'd otherwise be using different KMS keys.

```
iamRoleStatements:
  - Effect: Allow
    Action:
      - KMS:Decrypt
    Resource: ${env:KMS_KEY_ARN}
```

Once that is done, we can get the database password with a few lines of code to fetch the value and decrypt it into plaintext. The following code block shows how to decrypt the password, where the encrypted value is still being pulled out of the environment:

```
print("Decrypt the secret password")
client = boto3.client('kms')
binary_encrypted = base64.b64decode(os.environ['DB_PASSWORD'])
results = client.decrypt(CiphertextBlob=binary_encrypted)
db_password = results['Plaintext'].decode()
```

With that, we can now use the db_password value to connect to the database as usual.

There are a few things to take note of here. First, this adds a small bit of latency to your code since each call to decrypt is an API call to AWS; you can take advantage of the statefulness of warm functions and only perform the decryption if it hasn't already been done, using a global variable or some other application-level variable that can be initialized on startup. Second, once you have decrypted sensitive values like this, the onus is on you to not log them in plain text or otherwise advertise or record the plaintext values.

There are many things to consider when dealing with services such as KMS. This section is only a very brief introduction, and we've barely scratched the surface. I encourage you to read more about the subject and carefully think through how you can make your application as secure as you need to.

Trimming AWS Lambda versions

This last tip is specific to AWS Lambda. You may have noticed in other chapters that there are the following lines in the serverless.yml file:

```
plugins:
  - serverless-prune-plugin
```

By default, each time you deploy a new version of an AWS Lambda function, AWS will help out by keeping the old version around. In a development system where you may be deploying dozens of times a day, this can become quite wasteful and, as cheap as storage is, it's not unlimited. Also, in the case of a production system that has a lifetime of years, the cost of all the old versions can add up.

If you're using the Serverless Framework, there is an easy way around this. If you're not using the Serverless Framework, however, it would be no more than a day's work to write a small script to do this for you. The serverless-prune-plugin will keep only a certain number of Lambda versions for you and delete the rest. The number of versions to keep is configurable and trimming happens whenever you perform a full deployment. Additionally, you are given some nice CLI hooks to manually delete old versions. You can read the details about this plugin on its GitHub page: https://github.com/claygregory/serverless-prune-plugin.

If I add this to my previous divide function, configure the plugin to run automatically, and only keep two versions around, you can guess what will happen when I redeploy. That configuration I just mentioned will go into a custom block in my serverless.yml, shown as follows:

```
custom:
  prune:
    automatic: true
    number: 2
```

Next, I'll deploy my code to see the plugin prune the old versions for me. The following code block shows the output after running a full deployment, with some lines taken out for brevity:

```
# sls deploy -s dev
Serverless: Packaging service...
Serverless: Excluding development dependencies...
Serverless: Checking Stack update progress...
...................
Serverless: Stack update finished...
stack: error-handler-dev
api keys:
  None
endpoints:
  GET - https://3gz9zt2yv1.execute-api.us-west-2.amazonaws.com/dev
  GET - https://3gz9zt2yv1.execute-api.us-west-2.amazonaws.com/dev/process
functions:
  divide: error-handler-dev-divide
  process: error-handler-dev-process
Serverless: Prune: Running post-deployment pruning
Serverless: Prune: Querying for deployed versions
Serverless: Prune: error-handler-dev-divide has 11 additional versions
published and 0 aliases, 9 versions selected for deletion
Serverless: Prune: Deleting error-handler-dev-divide v9...
.....
Serverless: Prune: Deleting error-handler-dev-divide v1...
Serverless: Prune: error-handler-dev-process has 11 additional versions
published and 0 aliases, 9 versions selected for deletion
Serverless: Prune: Deleting error-handler-dev-process v9...
.....
Serverless: Prune: Deleting error-handler-dev-process v1...
Serverless: Prune: Pruning complete.
Serverless: Removing old service versions...
```

I recommend always using this plugin for AWS and Serverless Framework, as versioned Lambda functions aren't very useful. Another option is to simply disable function versioning completely. This can be accomplished by adding `versionFunctions: false` under the `provider` key in the `serverless.yml` file.

Summary

In this chapter, we covered general best practices when deploying serverless applications and error tracking. We looked at examples of how to integrate Rollbar and Sentry, two error tracking and reporting services, in AWS Lambda functions so that unexpected errors do not go unnoticed. We also discussed some strategies regarding application logging and methods to ensure you get the metrics and telemetry you need. We also addressed the issue of cold starts in cloud functions, and we discussed ways of working around them. From there, we walked through some techniques to help you with local testing and setting up serverless functions and systems. Finally, we reviewed the management of different environments or stacks using environment variables and the encryption of sensitive variables using AWS's Key Management Service.

Best practices for serverless applications could fill an entire book by themselves. We touched on many significant topics in this chapter that put you on the right trajectory moving forward. While this chapter cannot solve all of the challenges you may face in serverless application development, it does provide solutions to some of the most common issues and gives you the background necessary to find answers to your unique problems. At this point, readers should feel confident setting up and managing their own production-level serverless application.

Other Books You May Enjoy

If you enjoyed this book, you may be interested in these other books by Packt:

Building Serverless Architectures
Cagatay Gurturk

ISBN: 978-1-78712-919-1

- Learn to form microservices from bigger Softwares
- Orchestrate and scale microservices
- Design and set up the data flow between cloud services and custom business logic
- Get to grips with cloud provider's APIs, limitations, and known issues
- Migrate existing Java applications to a serverless architecture
- Acquire deployment strategies
- Build a highly available and scalable data persistence layer
- Unravel cost optimization techniques

Building Serverless Web Applications

Diego Zanon

ISBN: 978-1-78712-647-3

- Get a grasp of the pros and cons of going serverless and its use cases
- Discover how you can use the building blocks of AWS to your advantage
- Set up the environment and create a basic app with the Serverless Framework
- Host static files on S3 and CloudFront with HTTPS support
- Build a sample application with a frontend using React as an SPA
- Develop the Node.js backend to handle requests and connect to a SimpleDB database
- Secure your applications with authentication and authorization
- Implement the publish-subscribe pattern to handle notifications in a serverless application
- Create tests, define the workflow for deployment, and monitor your app

Leave a review - let other readers know what you think

Please share your thoughts on this book with others by leaving a review on the site that you bought it from. If you purchased the book from Amazon, please leave us an honest review on this book's Amazon page. This is vital so that other potential readers can see and use your unbiased opinion to make purchasing decisions, we can understand what our customers think about our products, and our authors can see your feedback on the title that they have worked with Packt to create. It will only take a few minutes of your time, but is valuable to other potential customers, our authors, and Packt. Thank you!

Index

A

Amazon Web Services (AWS) 19
Apigee
  reference 77
asynchronous processing, Twitter stream
  about 122
  data consumer 128, 131
  data producer 124
  results, viewing 133
  system architecture 122
AWS API Gateway 76
AWS Athena 187, 188, 189
AWS Certificate Manager (ACM) 20
AWS Lambda versions
  trimming 236
Azure Cosmos DB 145

B

batch layer
  about 142
  computation 146
benefits, queuing systems
  durability 118
  predictable load 118
  scalability 118
best practices, cold starts
  AWS Lambda functions 227
  cloud functions, working with 226
  memory allocation 228
  start-up times, for different languages 227
  VPCs 227
Big Data Benchmark dataset
  URL 187

C

cold starts 226
complex integration
  application code, implementing 94
  Lambda function, using 93
  new resource and method, setting up 96
content delivery network (CDN) 19
cryptocurrency prices, processing
  AWS resources 149, 151, 152, 154
  batch layer 158, 161, 162
  data producer 154, 156
  lambda architecture, using 146
  results 162, 164
  speed layer 156, 158
  system architecture 147

D

data layer, three-tier web application with REST 30
data producers
  streaming 144
data storage 144, 145
data store
  using, for results 190, 191
dead-letter queue
  using 137
deployed web application
  viewing 43
DynamoDB 145

E

Elastic MapReduce (EMR)
  using 191
Enron emails, processing
  datasets, URL 175
  driver function, implementing 176, 177, 178

mapper, implementing 178, 180
reducer, implementing 180, 181, 183, 184
with serverless MapReduce 175
environments
  managing 231
error tracking
  about 216
  Rollbar, integrating 222
  Sentry, integrating into 217, 221

F

fanout pattern
  using, with messaging pattern 134
Firehose
  reference 161

G

Google Bigtable 145
GraphQL
  about 52
  reference 56

I

images, resizing
  about 104
  application code, implementing 107, 109
  code, testing 110
  permissions, setting up 106
  project, setting up 104
  trigger, setting up 105
  worker functions, setting up 105

J

JsonPlaceholder
  reference 77

K

Kinesis Firehose stream
  reference 152
Kong
  reference 77

L

lambda architecture
  about 140
  batch layer 142
  cryptocurrency prices, processing 146
  examples 140, 142
  reference 140
  speed layer 143
Lambda function
  used, for complex integration 93
lambda serverless architecture
  about 143
  batch layer, computation 146
  data producers, streaming 144
  data storage 144, 145
  speed layer, computation 145
local development 228
log messages
  structuring 223
logging systems 223
Loggly
  reference 225
logic layer, three-tier web application 59
logic layer, three-tier web application with GraphQL
  application code, organizing 56
  function layout 57
  Lambda functions, organizing 54
  mutations, implementing 63
  queries, implementing 60
  writing 58
logic layer, three-tier web application with REST
  andler.py, wiring to Lambda via API Gateway 36
  application code and function layout 23
  application code, organizing 25
  application entrypoint 31
  application logic 33
  code structure 26
  configuration with environment variables 26
  function layout 28
  Lambda functions, organizing 24
  writing 30

M

mapper
  role 170
MapReduce
  about 167
  architecture 171, 173
  benefits 168
  example 169, 170
  mapper, role 170
  reducer, role 171
  references 168
  serverless architecture 173, 175
messaging pattern
  using, with fanout pattern 134
migration
  staged migration 98
  techniques 97
  URLs, migrating 99

N

notifications
  using, with queues 115
  using, with subscriptions 113

P

pass-through proxy
  deploying 81
  setting up 78
points of presence (POPs) 30
Postgres database
  deploying 39
presentation layer, three-tier web application with
    REST
  about 29
  CDN with CloudFront 30
  file storage with S3 29
proxy integration 76
proxy resource 98
proxy
  applying, to legacy API 77
pyrollbar
  reference 222

Q

queue
  notifications, using 115
  using, as rate-limiter 135
queuing systems
  about 118
  benefits 118
  queue service, selecting 119
  queues, versus streams 120

R

reducer
  role 171
response transformation
  example, setting 86
  Integration Request, setting up 88
  Integration Response, setting up 91
  method execution flow 84
  method, setting up 87
  resource, setting up 87
responses
  transforming, from modern API 83
REST API
  deploying 37
Rollbar
  integrating 222

S

sensitive configuration
  securing 232
  variables, decrypting 235
  variables, encrypting 233
Sentry
  integrating, for error tracking 216, 221
serverless frameworks
  reference 20
serverless functions
  daemon processes, mimicking 126
serverless MapReduce, alternatives
  AWS Athena 187, 188, 189
  data store, using for results 190, 191
  Elastic MapReduce (EMR), using 191
  exploring 187
serverless MapReduce, limitations

about 185
   memory limits 185
   storage limits 186
   time limits 187
serverless MapReduce
   architecture 173, 175
   for processing Enron emails 175
serverless tooling 20
serverless-prune-plugin
   reference 236
Simple Notification Service (SNS) 113
Simple Queuing Service (SQS) 115
Simple Storage Service (S3) 29
speed layer
   about 143
   computation 145
staged migration 98
static assets
   setting up 41
streaming systems
   AWS 144
   Azure 144
   Google Compute Cloud 144
structured logs
   digesting 225
subscriptions
   notifications, using 113
system architecture, cryptocurrency price
   processing
   about 147
   batch layer 148
   data producer 148
   speed layer 148

system architecture
   about 102
   synchronous invocation, versus asynchronous
      invocation 103

T

testing
   local method 229
tests
   executing 44
three-tier web application, with GraphQL
   deployed application, viewing 66
   deployment 64
   iteration and deployment 72
   logic layer 54
   logic layer, working with 58
   presentation layer 57
   system architecture 53
three-tier web application, with REST
   about 23
   code, deploying 48
   data layer 23
   entire stack, deploying 47
   iteration and deployment 47
   logic layer 23
   presentation layer 23
   system architecture 21
Twelve-Factor App
   reference 26

V

virtual private cloud (VPC) 40

Printed in Great Britain
by Amazon